Indiana and the *Sultana* Disaster; The Story of a Survivor

This book chronicles numerous events, people and places from the 1831 birth of John H. King to his death in 1893.

By Robert R. Smith

Published & distributed by:
Robert R. Smith

in association with:
IBJ Book Publishing, LLC.
41 E. Washington St., Suite 200
Indianapolis, IN 46204
www.ibjbp.com

Library of Congress Control Number: 2015948276
ISBN 978-1-939550-24-8
First Edition
Printed in the United States of America

A Timeline to Tragedy:

Chapter 1
Destiny Begins

In 1831, the year John Henry King was born, Cincinnati, Ohio was still a new city. It was a city that symbolized a young and growing America. Democrat Andrew Jackson was President of the United States, and the emerging Ohio River community had appointed Elisha Hotchkiss, a member of the Whig party, as their second mayor.

That same year Mr. John H. Wood published the first issue of the *Cincinnati Mirror*, an eight-page semi-monthly newspaper for the local residents. The new and developing city was a composite of people representing every class in society who came together in search of something new and with hope for a better life.[1]

The Kings, young John Henry's family, were among the growing city's common people, working and raising families in those early pioneering days. Mr. George King, John Henry's father, and his wife Louisa had moved west from the state of Maryland to Cincinnati where George set up a blacksmithing business and began practicing his trade.[2]

In those early days of the Riverboat City it was common for young boys to follow in the footsteps of their fathers' occupation, usually starting before the boys reached their teenage years. In the profession of blacksmithing, a young apprentice would begin with the very basics of his father's trade: starting and stoking the fire, disposing of the ashes, filling and changing the water bucket, and tending to the inventory materials of iron, wood, coal, horseshoes and nails, hammers, and tongs, all the necessary tools and supplies needed to run an efficient shop.

After serving his time doing all of the small, but necessary, things and with the approval of his father, the apprentice would move on to the finer parts of the trade by learning and understanding the art of the profession. He was taught how to use the bellows to control the fire, how to use the various areas and angles of the anvil for shaping each project, which hammer to use for the shaping, when and how to use the tongs, and the proper use of the vice. Over time, with many days of practice and tutoring, the apprentice would learn the intricacies of the trade and would master the skill of knowing when the metal had reached the proper malleability by the color of the heated metal. At that point the apprentice had reached the goals set by both himself and his father for his apprenticeship.

In the 1840s, blacksmithing was far more than simply shoeing horses. People went to the Kings' blacksmith shop for things they needed that were not available at local stores. A skilled craftsman for instance could build wagons, make bridle bits, farm implements and tools, household utensils, locks, hinges, and just about any other item requested by neighbors and local businessmen.[3] Young John continued working with and learning from his father as a blacksmith's apprentice until finally reaching the point when he felt competent. Confident enough of his newly acquired skills to make a decision to leave Cincinnati and begin life on his own. So, the young and enthusiastic John King followed the pioneer obsession of that period and headed west across the Ohio state line into Indiana.

Chapter 2

The Raymonds and the Van Camps

Thomas Raymond and his wife Amey (Flewelling) Raymond were one of the many families who made the move west to Indiana. They were among the very early families who settled in Franklin County, having moved there from Nine Partners in Dutchess County, New York around 1830. After their arrival, the family settled into a home on Duck Creek in Metamora Township, Franklin County. Amey and Thomas had eleven children, four of whom died in infancy before Amey's death in 1840.[4] Two of those children were Hester, born in July of 1828 in New York, and Katherine, born in Franklin County, Indiana in October of 1833. Although the sisters would remain close throughout their lives one would lead a life of prosperity, and the other a life of misfortune.[5]

At the age of 21, Hester, the eldest of the two sisters, married 32-year-old Gilbert Van Camp. They were married on October 15, 1849 in Franklin County, Indiana shortly after Gilbert's first wife, Mary Ann (Gregg), died.[6]

Gilbert's father, Charles M. Van Camp, born May 12, 1787, whose own father had been a Captain of Volunteers in the War of the Revolution, moved from New Jersey to the Indiana territory around 1804. He was an early pioneer in Dearborn County, establishing himself in the area as a farmer and wagon maker. Charles worked hard on his farm for the next twelve years before meeting and marrying Mary Halstead, whose family had migrated to Indiana from New York. They were married on December 12, 1816, one day after Indiana received statehood.

On Christmas day of the following year, Mary gave birth to their son Gilbert in Brookville, Franklin County, Indiana, where they were now living.

While Gilbert was growing up, he worked with his father on the family farm, putting in long, hard, hot, tedious, and routine days. However, the imaginative young man wanted more for himself than the life of a farmer, so in 1833, at age 17, he left home to seek his own way in life. He quickly found a job as a Miller's apprentice. After four hard-working and hard-learning years, he had saved enough money to form a partnership with Mr. John H. Fudge, a local tinsmith.

The two of them set up a business to sell stoves and tin ware in the town of Brookville. Gilbert's ambitious nature led him to learn everything he could, so he took advantage of his time while operating and managing the Fudge & Van Camp store to improve his knowledge and expertise. Part of that on-the-job training was to learn and develop the skills of tinsmithing from his new partner.

In 1853 the ever-resourceful and confident young businessman decided he wanted to own and operate his own business despite his success with the Fudge & Van Camp store. Gilbert made a difficult choice and parted ways with his mentor and partner, Mr. Fudge. His plan was to move Hester and their two children— Mary, age three, and Courtland, who was not quite a year old—to Greensburg, Indiana, where he wanted to open a stove and tin store under the Van Camp name.[7]

While Hester and Gilbert were making their plans, Hester's

sister Katherine, age 19, had completed her schooling and was still living at home. With the prospect of continuing a boring and lonely existence living with her father, her sister's new adventure sounded very appealing and she decided to make the move with the young couple to Greensburg. John Raymond, a younger brother of Hester and Katherine, also joined his siblings in the move.

Now numbering a total of six family members, the group made the journey southwest from Franklin County and across the border into adjacent Decatur County and into the small town of Greensburg.

It was 1853 and the population of Greensburg had grown to 1,200 citizens. The local commerce consisted of seven blacksmith shops, employing a total of seventeen men; four wagon shops employing ten men; four shoe shops with eight men; two cabinet shops; two tan yards where animal hides were processed into leather; and two carding machines, used to prepare fiber materials for the production of textiles.

The main street in Greensburg had an ordinance limiting the speed of all vehicles to four miles an hour, and excessive speed resulted in the substantial fine of one dollar. Hogs ran loose in the downtown area and for their pleasure and convenience mud holes were provided on the streets surrounding the square. It was a common occurrence to see the hogs rooting for grubs on the courthouse lawn. The situation improved in 1861 when a law was passed requiring owners to put rings in the snouts of their hogs.[8]

After settling in, Gilbert, Hester, and her two siblings, Katherine and John Raymond, began to prepare for the opening of Greenfield's new stove and tin store. Gilbert had acquired a prime spot on the southwest corner of the public square and was now in the process of creating his dream. His brother-in-law, John Raymond assisted Gilbert with the preparations. When the store was ready to open, he took on the role of apprentice tinsmith in the town's newest business.[9]

During her first year in the city of Greensburg, Decatur County, Katherine met a young blacksmith by the name of John H. King who had settled in Greensburg after moving from his former home in Cincinnati. Since some of Gilbert's work, such as making dog irons (fireplace inserts for holding logs of wood) and sad irons (also called flat irons or smoothing irons), was often jobbed out, it's possible that a young John H. King was working through a local blacksmith for Gilbert giving him the opportunity to meet the young Miss Katherine Raymond.

Van Camp Ad, February 12 of 1856

John Henry King and Katherine Raymond began a brief courtship and on June 5, 1854, the same year the now-famous courthouse with the tree began construction, the two were married.[10] The following month, Hester Van Camp gave birth to a son, Edgar Van Camp, again expanding the Raymond and Van Camp families.[11]

In July of 1855, Katherine and John King became parents with the birth of their first child, a son whom they named Wesley.[12] A child who would later help his mother through many difficult times.

While the Kings were adjusting their lives to accommodate their new family member, some notable events were taking place in the state of Indiana. Just 57 miles to the northwest of Greensburg William Conner died on August 28, 1855 in Noblesville, Indiana. Conner had moved to the Indiana territory from Tuscarawas County, Ohio as a young man during the winter of 1800–1801. The land he purchased was in an area that had been recently established by Congress and was given the name "Indiana Territory," or "Land of Indians."

Conner settled in a still-wild area on the east bank of the White River that was populated with dense forest and the Lenape (pronounced len-AH-pay) or Delaware Indians. This land was just a little northwest of what would later become Fishers Switch and due south of the town of Noblesville. Conner would become a landowner, trader, interpreter, scout, community leader, and entrepreneur while living in this area.

In 1823, at the age of 43, Conner built an impressive home for his 18-year-old Indian wife. The ornately furnished brick house he'd built, buried in the wilderness, stood in sharp contrast to its surroundings.

The couple would raise seven of their ten children in that home. Conner and his family lived there until moving to Noblesville in 1837, feeling that the area had made a transition from wilderness to a more settled and populated setting. He died eighteen years later.

The footpaths he helped create turned into roads, and the forests surrounding his land had been cut back as the growing towns and settlements in the area continued to spread.[13]

Fortunately for history and historical preservation the Conners' land, house, and accompanying heritage were purchased in 1934 by Eli Lilly, a man of vision who understood their importance. It was to be the first step in the shaping of today's Conner Prairie living history museum.

The same year that William Conner died, 50 miles to the northwest of the Kings' and Van Camps' homes in Greensburg, the opportunity for higher education increased in Indianapolis. On November 1, 1855, attorney and abolitionist Ovid Butler opened the doors of a new university at 13ᵗʰ Street and College Avenue. The North Western Christian University was a fully co-educational school capable of handling around 300 students in a four-story stone-and-brick building that was set on 25 acres of native Indiana trees. The school would later become Butler University.[14]

By the mid-1850's the Kings and the Van Camps had become a recognized part of the Greensburg community, comfortable with their new life adventures in the growing town. The Van Camp family business was doing well enough to afford an advertisement in the local newspaper. On February 12, 1856, Gilbert placed an ad on page three of the *Decatur County Republican* featuring the latest line of stoves, brass kettles, tin ware, skillets, fruit cans of three different sizes, odd lids, sad irons, and dog irons. His personal services included job work in tin, copper or sheet iron that could be "Done on Short Notice."[15]

In the 1850s, life was anything but predictable. Good fortune and tragedy were equal partners. Just six months following Wesley's birth, the two families were shocked when a tragedy occurred on January 3, 1857. Gilbert and Hester's young son, Edgar Van Camp, then only two years and seven months old, died. The cause of death was listed as "cutting teeth." He was buried in South Park Cemetery (originally Decatur County Cemetery), Lot 65, Grave 1.

The local doctor in charge of treating Edgar, John H. Alexander, was recognized by the locals as a very successful and competent practitioner of the medical profession. During his college years Dr. Alexander was an avid reader of medical texts and journals, furthering his competency and knowledge prior to his graduation from the Ohio Medical College.

Despite his best efforts, medical knowledge at that time was still extremely limited. Little Edgar Van Camp could not be saved.[16]

In 1859, Gilbert took on a partner in his growing business.

The March 21 issue of the *Decatur Press* posted an ad for the newly named Phares Van Camp Stove and Tin Store, still located on the southeast corner of the square across from the Moss House, which was a livery and feed store. Isaac T. Phares had the official job title of clerk, but the 1860 census shows that he had a personal estate of $4,000 and personal real estate valued at $1,400, so it is likely that he was a clerk with some ownership in the business. The Phares family was well known in Shelby and Decatur counties. They were a family of Baptist ministers who circuited the area holding Church services for the locals.[17]

On May 21, 1860, another tragedy occurred, this time touching the lives of the King family. Word was received that a two-mile wide tornado tore through John's hometown of Cincinnati, inundating the city with a torrential rain, severe thunder, and lightning. The force of the wind ripped up trees by the roots; flattened buildings; tore the roofs off homes, offices, and churches; and destroyed telegraph lines. The massive debris was enough to block the city's railroad tracks.

When the tornado hit the Ohio River, it attacked the city's shoreline, sinking steamboats and other vessels as it continued up the Ohio River.

Two miles north of the city, the steamer Virginia Home was capsized, and the cabin parted from the hull and floated down the river in fragments. There were only three passengers on board, and all were saved. Two of the crew were lost.

The same storm had come in from the northwest and hit portions of Indiana and Kentucky, as well. In Madison, Indiana, six or eight buildings were unroofed and three of four pairs of coal boats were sunk—six men went missing. The steamer Eunice was damaged near Ghent, Kentucky, as well. Her cabin and chimneys were blown overboard, as well as a portion of her freight. The steamer Argyle lost her chimneys. Wharf boats at Patriot, Chent, and Carrollton were ripped from their moorings and the wreckage carried down stream.

The destruction done to Cincinnati was immense. The physical damage was estimated at half a million dollars. The number of people injured was huge, but early reports said only six people were killed. Newspapers at the time said it was the most destructive tornado ever known to hit the city.[18]

When the news of the Cincinnati tornado reached Greensburg, Indiana, John King certainly had reason for concern. Current news arrived on a time delay and details were limited leaving John with absolutely no information on the welfare of his Ohio-based family.

He had not seen his family for several years and he now had a new wife and young son to introduce to his relatives. John made the decision that he would return home, so he and Katherine packed up their belongings, bundled up little Wesley, and headed east.[19]

John King's brother-in-law Gilbert had now been doing business in Greensburg for nearly seven years when a new business opportunity arose around the same time the Kings left for Ohio. He received an offer to work with Indianapolis farmer and businessman Martin Williams on a project financed by entrepreneur Calvin Fletcher. The chance to move to Indianapolis and work on such a major project was just too much for Gilbert to pass up, so he packed up his family—now with two additional children — Ella and Clara — and moved to Indianapolis in July of 1860.[20]

When the Kings left for Cincinnati and the Van Camps moved to Indianapolis, John Raymond, Gilbert's brother-in-law, stayed behind, taking over Gilbert's corner site on the square in downtown Greensburg and began running his own hardware business in the same location as the Van Camp store.[21]

John Raymond was most certainly a caring and optimistic soul.

In 1863, he married Josephine Hilles, and the newlyweds took in Josephine's sister, Mary Hazelrigg, and her five-year-old son, Scott, when Mary's husband, J.F. Hazelrigg, died. Young Scott Hazelrigg would live a highly regarded life, eventually leaving Indiana and becoming so prominent that he was listed in the January 1903 issue of *The Successful American*.

His resume included being General Manager of the Atlantic Coast Electric Railroad Company, Vice President and General Manager of the Richmond Light and Railroad Company, Vice-President and General Manager of the Staten Island Midland Railroad Company, President and General Manager of the New Jersey & Staten Island Ferry Company and President of the Southfield Beach Railroad.[22]

When the Van Camps were settled in the capitol city of Indianapolis, Gilbert and his new partner began their plans to design and build a cold storage warehouse for perishable foods. The first order of business for Gilbert and Mr. Williams was to find and purchase land near the downtown area. They settled on a site on the north side of Ohio Street between the Canal and West Street and began building their new facility.

After nearly a year of working, planning, and experimenting, the storage unit was finally complete. It had three-foot thick walls filled with straw and lined with galvanized iron to insulate it. To further enhance the insulation, the builders covered the entire unit with sheet iron. Their prototype proved very successful and the new innovative design was eventually used for household iceboxes and refrigerated train cars.[23]

As the project began drawing to a close, Gilbert began considering his next venture, which he hoped would be more long term and provide financial stability for himself and his family.

While living in Greensburg, Gilbert was aware of a successful business owned by H.D. and W.W. Pope that sold freshly canned fruits. The Pope Canned Fruits building was located on Gibson's Corner where customers visiting the store could purchase canned peaches, pineapple, apples, and other fruits. It is very likely that Gilbert provided the Popes with the tin cans used for storing the fruits since the Popes' ad in the *Decatur Republican* offered three sizes of fruit cans. Whether or not the Pope's store was Gilbert's inspiration for his next project, he decided on a similar plan for his next endeavor.[24]

He shared his idea of canning and selling fruit with Martin Williams, his partner from the storage unit project. Williams was an eminent farmer and fruit grower with a large farm just northwest of the city. Gilbert suggested that Williams not only be a partner in the business, but that they should also buy and use the fruit from his farm. Williams agreed to a partnership, and Gilbert was soon sharing the exciting news with Hester.

The two of them began working together to design and test the canning process. Hester prepared the fruit, Gilbert made the containers, and the two of them did the canning.[25] The process was not easy. While Hester worked through the day and into the evening cooking and canning, Gilbert used his tinsmith skills to make quart and six-gallon size canisters to hold and store the fruits. He also made the pots that Hester used for cooking.

When they had a sufficient stockpile of canned goods, he and Hester started selling the finished product to friends, neighbors, and relatives out of a shed in the backyard of their home at 112 North Missouri Street.[26]

The canned fruits were an immediate success and the word spread quickly. Hardworking housewives and mothers were now able to quickly prepare the canned goods without spending hours in the kitchen, providing a little bit of treasured time for themselves.

With Williams's support, the Van Camps soon moved out of their backyard operation and into a retail space at 110 West Ohio Street, just north of the local paper mill. Williams and the Van Camps were now in operation and began business as the "Fruit House".[27]

By this time, John and Katherine King had settled in Cincinnati and were living with his father and mother in the southern part of the city on Western Row, between 4th and 5th.[28]

The devastated city was now united in rebuilding from the disastrous storm and the young King family settled into their new surroundings where John's family welcomed Katherine and young grandson Wesley.

Chapter 3

Indiana and the Onset of the Civil War

While the Kings and the Van Camps were adjusting to the changes in their lives the country was experiencing difficult times. The conflict between the northern states and the seceding southern states had nearly reached its peak. The country was at odds over economic conflicts and political theories and there was an increasing emotional rise of irreconcilable differences on both sides of the issues.

The main concern was the economy. The South was almost entirely a farming region with few factories. The major crops were tobacco and cotton, which were sold worldwide, and slave labor was essential to the production of these crops. At the beginning of the Civil War more than a third of the Southern population was black, establishing the three and a half million slaves as the mainstay of the South's prosperity.

Although prejudice against African Americans at that time was nationwide, the North, whose economic base was in factory work, did not incorporate slave labor into its workforce. Eventually, the North established a group of abolitionists who began calling for an end to slavery. When Abraham Lincoln was voted in as a member of the abolitionist Republican Party in 1860, the South saw this as the beginning of the end for their Southern culture and economy.[29]

Even before Lincoln was sworn in as the new President, U.S. soldiers stationed in Charleston, South Carolina, were already being called "the enemy" by the local citizens.

Major Robert Anderson was in command of the U.S. troops in that area and oversaw the three military forts located around the Charleston Harbor. His second in command was Captain Abner Doubleday, who has often been credited with the development of the game of baseball even though historians who examined the evidence stripped him of this honor.

Also stationed at Charleston was an Indiana soldier who unfortunately had the same name as the man who would become president of the Confederacy, Jefferson C. Davis. The Indiana man was born in Clark County, Indiana and was now serving as officer of the guard.[30]

As tensions increased in the city of Charleston, Major Anderson feared for the safety of his men and their families. He was working from Fort Moultrie and was convinced that the garrison was indefensible because it had been built for the War of 1812 and had been badly neglected for years. After giving serious consideration to what would be best for his men and their families he decided to move everyone to Fort Sumter and make that his base of operations. He considered Sumter a much better site to defend in the event of an attack from the locals and the Southern militiamen.

Before Anderson decided to make this move to the new fort, South Carolina seceded from the Union on December 12, 1860. Suddenly the local militia was now keeping a much closer eye on the actions of Union troops in and around Charleston.

Major Anderson assumed, correctly, that the local Militiamen also knew that Fort Sumter was more defensible so he developed a plan to mislead the local troops and spread word that the families of his men would be moving to the old, unoccupied Fort Johnson where they would be safe.

The day after Christmas, Major Anderson, his troops, and their families moved out in six large oared boats pretending they were going to Fort Johnson, which was a short distance past Fort Sumter.

As they approached Fort Sumter, they quickly changed direction and made a dash for the docking area adjacent to the fort. They landed safely and immediately began to prepare for an attack.

The Southerners were furious. They had been claiming that Fort Sumter rightly belonged to South Carolina now that the state had seceded. In response, the southern Militiamen took over Fort Moultrie, Anderson's previous base of operations, and Castle Pinckney, the other Union fort in the area.

Accusations and threats continued for months between the two adversaries while more Southern states seceded in support.

The standoff finally ended when Confederate General Pierre Beauregard sent a boat containing two of his aides to Fort Sumter under a white flag of truce so that they could present a message to Major Anderson demanding the evacuation of the fort. Major Anderson refused and the aides headed back to Beauregard with the distressing news.

The aides returned to Fort Sumter on April 12 at 12:45 a.m. and asked Major Anderson how long he thought his men could hold out. After conferring with his officers on this matter, Anderson presented Beauregard's aides with a list of demands and promised that, if they were met, his troops would evacuate the fort on April 15.

Beauregard was prepared for this response and the messengers replied to the demands with a written statement that the terms were unacceptable and that, by order of General Beauregard, Southern troops would open fire on Fort Sumter in one hour.

That same day, April 12, 1861, the Confederates made good on the promise.

It was recorded that when the first shot was fired at Fort Sumter, it sailed right over the head of Hoosier Lieutenant Jefferson C. Davis of the 1st Artillery.

The offensive blitz was devastating. After taking 600 direct hits to the fort and its troops, the overmatched Union troops surrendered the fort. The war between the North and the South had begun.[31]

Prior to the attack, attorney and statesman Lew Wallace, who was the son of a former Indiana Governor, met with the current Governor Oliver Morton to share information he'd overheard in a secret meeting held by local Democrats. He informed the governor that the South may attempt to force secession and promised him, "If these leaders are right, Governor, and the South does attempt forcible secession, I tender you my services in advance. You may command me absolutely."

With tearing eyes, the governor responded, "You could not go with the South, or with any treasonable organization here at home. That is not in your blood. I tell you also in advance: if the South goes to the extreme of war or threatens it by any overt act, I will send for you, first man."

On the afternoon of April 13, the day after the firing on Fort Sumter, Wallace was addressing a jury in the Clinton County Circuit Court in Indiana when the telegraph operator of the town ran into the court room and told the judge he had a telegram for Wallace. The judge nodded to the sheriff, who gave the note to Wallace.

The message read

Sumter has been fired on. Come immediately.

OLIVER P. MORTON.

Wallace had been called into action. The governor had been true to his word. Wallace arrived around 7:00 a.m. the next morning, which was a Sunday, and learned the governor was already in his office. Governor Morton welcomed him and said, "The firing on Sumter is the overt act I have been expecting for some days. Mr. Lincoln has now no resort except to suppress the treason by force. He must call for troops.

"In fact, he has notified me of such an intention, and to answer for Indiana, I sent for you. I want you to become Adjutant General. The president will call immediately for seventy-five thousand men, and the quota of Indiana will be six regiments.

I want those regiments raised without the loss of an hour. What do you say?" Wallace agreed and asked that he also be able to command one of the new units.

In the next seven days, over three times the number of men required to fill Indiana's quota for the president's call offered their services to the country and Adjutant General Lew Wallace began his plan to form his 11th Zouave Regiment.[32] Zouave units traditionally wore uniforms which included short open-fronted jackets, baggy trousers, and often sashes and tasseled head gear.

When the events at Fort Sumter, the declaration of war, and the call for troops hit the local newspapers, alarmed Hoosiers began enlisting at an impressive pace. Posters calling for men to enlist began appearing everywhere. Urgent headlines declared, "Patriots Your Country Needs You," "The Union Forever," and "Soldiers Wanted!" Hoards of angry and determined men rushed to join the battle to protect their families and support the principles of the Northern states.

Other Indiana men withheld their commitment due to family,

religion, indecision, or just plain indifference. Some decided to wait and see how the war progressed before making their pledges of allegiance.

One concerned Indiana citizen was Herman Sturm. Sturm had come to Indiana from Hanover, Germany, whose was a maker of fine surveying, navigation, and drawing instruments. He had also studied the process of manufacturing ammunition while he lived in Europe. In 1861, he was living in Franklin, Indiana with his wife Anna, his children—Henrietta, who was six, Henry, who was three, and George, who was one—along with his sixty-year-old father, Henry Sturm.

After hearing the Union Army was under-supplied in munitions, early in 1861 he set to work in his home testing the process of making cartridges. When he was satisfied with the quality of his product he approached Governor Morton with samples of his work and offered his services as a munitions expert.

The governor recognized the importance and the quality of the munitions Sturm presented but informed Sturm that he could not immediately move forward without the sanction of the federal legislature.

Undeterred, Sturm approached a group of Indianapolis Bankers. They also recognized the value of his proposal and agreed to finance the project. When Governor Morton was informed of the financial backing, he quickly arranged for Sturm to go to Washington and personally present his product and his plan.

After reviewing the proposal, learning of the financing, and seeing the quality of Sturm's munitions, he received approval from the U.S. Federal Ordnance Department.

Immediately upon Sturm's return on April 27, 1861 the

plan was put into action. A temporary state arsenal was built on government property just north of the State House, running from Market to Ohio Street. The mission was to supply munitions of war to Indiana Regiments. Sturm would supervise the entire operation and was named a Captain of the Ordinance Department. Amazingly the arsenal was ready to open and began operations in just ten days. The process began and the ammunition flowed. Sturm's hope for an Indiana arsenal was complete. The arsenal later moved to Sturm's personal property and then moved a second time to 1500 E. Michigan Street; in 1912 the one time Arsenal became Arsenal Technical High School.[33]

Around the same time Sturm began his arsenal efforts in Indianapolis an exciting event took place in the still small city of Greensburg, Indiana.

On February 12, 1861, newly elected President Abraham Lincoln arrived in the city by train, stopping briefly on his way to assume the presidency in Washington. Two thousand citizens assembled in the area to give a warm greeting to their new leader. It was the President's birthday, so the stop was brief. Lincoln did not have time to make a speech but he thanked those in attendance and asked for music "that, of course, would reflect the sentiment and strong favor of the Union." The crowd sang "The Flag of Our Union" and then the local brass band struck up "Hail, Columbia." Local resident John Doakes, a member of the Republican political club "Wide-Awakes," presented the president-elect with a very large, nice apple. Lincoln graciously accepted and the train departed for Cincinnati and the nation's capital.

Lincoln made a previous stop in Greensburg when the Kings and the Van Camps were still living in that city. The date of the visit was September 19, 1859—the same year Greensburg became a city. Lincoln was on his way home to Illinois after campaigning in Cincinnati and arrived in the city around 3 p.m. The local newspaper, *The Republican*, reported that a large number of citizens greeted the candidate as flags were fluttering and music from brass instruments resounded through the air. Although it is unknown what Lincoln said to the large gathering, it was most likely something similar to speeches he'd made at other stops along the way.

He was quoted in other Indiana papers as telling crowds that as he traveled through Indiana, his thoughts were carried back to the time his father brought him from Kentucky to Indiana when he was eight years old. He also talked about what he had learned during his pioneer days in Indiana and repeated what he had said so often in his speeches, "This government can not endure permanently, half slave and half free."

Eventually, railroad and whistle-stop political campaigning became a regular part of American life, but this early stop in Greensburg may very well have been among the first presidential whistle stops in the country.[34]

In Cincinnati, John King was busy resettling his family and aware of the troubling circumstances facing the divided nation. Many of the locals rushed to enlist for the sake of the Union. But Katherine was now five months pregnant and leaving his wife and four-year-old son was not an option.[35]

Men of all nationalities, sizes, and ages continued to sign up for the cause creating a very diverse group of soldiers. There were farmers, white-collar workers, laborers, politicians, and former military men in this collection of new enlistees. Most were men between eighteen and twenty-nine, but there was a fair share of middle-aged and older men, as well.

As men from all areas of the North began to join up, Indiana led the way in enlistment oddities. Believing the war would not last long, men from Indiana were anxious to enlist before the conflict ended. The recruiting attracted young, old, and odd. One Indianapolis man had shaved his beard and dyed his hair to be accepted. Shoe cobbler Peter Kopp, who was over six feet tall, recruited men for the 27th Indiana Monroe County Grenadiers but did not accept anyone under five feet, ten inches tall. His prize recruit and co-organizer was David Van Buskirk from near Gosport, Indiana. He stood six feet, ten and a half inches tall. Records kept by the War Department Archives in Washington, DC officially named Buskirk "The biggest man to wear the Union uniform." One Indianapolis man was mustered in even though he was ninety-two years old. The Home Guard had a unit called the "Silver Grays" that was captained by seventy-year-old James Blake.[36]

The Federal minimum age limit for enlisting was set at eighteen, but a number of younger soldiers in Indiana were accepted because they lied about their age. Some were able to convince their parents to give permission to join the frenzy of enlistments. Parents would occasionally give permission since a new enlistee would get a sign-up bonus of around $300. and a monthly paycheck of $13-a decent amount of money in those difficult times.[37]

The really young enlistees were usually accepted as musicians or drummer boys, but regardless of age, they were sent into battle with their respective units. Most of the younger enlistees were in their early teens, but Edward Black set the record for both the

North and South when he enlisted in Indianapolis at the age of eight years and six months. He was assigned to be a drummer boy to Company L of the 21st Indiana Volunteer Infantry. General N. P. Banks later changed the Regiment's name to "First Heavy Artillery" in February 1863.

From then until it was mustered out in 1865, the regiment served in several locations around the Gulf.

The young drummer boy went with his unit when the 21st Infantry was sent to seize New Orleans, Louisiana in May of 1862 and was captured at the August 5, 1862 Battle of Baton Rouge. Fifteen days later, he was freed with other Union prisoners when the city surrendered to the Union on August 20, 1862, and the young drummer boy marched with his regimental band into the captured city.[38]

During the month of August, before that Baton Rouge surrender, young Wesley King celebrated his sixth birthday, making him just a couple of years shy of Edward Black's enlistment age, but Wesley had been doing some traveling of his own. For the first few years of their lives together, John and Katherine, despite having a young child and the logistics and extreme difficulties of long-distance travel, made their home in both Indiana and Ohio.

While still living in Cincinnati, the Kings' second child, Nettie, was born in September of 1861. Shortly thereafter John and Katherine began making plans to return to Indiana.[39] Katherine was more than pleased with this decision, because they were moving to Indianapolis and she could once again be near her older sister Hester. Despite the turmoil of the war, having two young children, and the exhausting, somewhat dangerous ordeal of moving, the King family headed back to Indiana. When they arrived in Indianapolis, the Kings moved into a home at 107 East Ohio Street.

At that time, Hester and Gilbert lived just down the street from the Fruit House at 110 West Ohio Street.[40]

The same year that the Kings returned to Indiana, General Lew Wallace, now commanding the Third Division of the Army of Tennessee under Ulysses S. Grant, was at Crump's Landing in Tennessee where he had been assigned to destroy the tracks of the Mobile and Ohio Railroad. On April 6, 1862, Wallace received a desperate message from General Grant ordering him to proceed to Shiloh, which was about six miles to the south. There were two possible routes to the site, and the one Wallace chose was a mistake. He and his troops arrived six hours later than expected. When they arrived, the unit he was sent to support was gone and the battle was over. In the aftermath, there was a dispute over the wording in the orders from Grant. Wallace claimed one version of the letter and Grant another. The actual written orders, which would have resolved the matter, were lost during the march to Shiloh. Grant was furious.

At the end of the battle, Shiloh became the bloodiest conflict of the Civil War to that date. Grant never forgave Wallace, despite his sterling military career.

Fatalities from the clash between the two armies at Shiloh numbered at over 10,000 men on each side. With the possible exceptions of Antietam and Gettysburg, this battle has been the subject of more controversy than any other Civil War battle.[41]

As the war raged on, John King returned to his work as a blacksmith. Katherine, once again pregnant, minded the home and their two young children. In May of 1862, Katherine gave birth to a new son. George Wallace King joined his brother Wesley and sister Nettie as part of the growing King family.[42]

The new child added another reason to John's enlistment decision. Enlisting would now mean leaving behind his wife, his two young children, and an infant son. It would mean giving up a civilian life and his job as a blacksmith and marching off to a frightening and unknown future. He may have felt the need to help his country, but the painful emotional and financial consequences of leaving his family would have been too much.

Chapter 4

Eli Lilly

Eli Lilly was another young man in Indiana at that time with a decision to make. Lilly, who was living in Greencastle, Indiana while the war was heating up, had spent two years at Asbury College, modern-day's DePauw University, studying Pharmacology before moving to Lafayette, Indiana and then settling in Greencastle. The move to Lafayette was a career decision. He worked at the Good Samaritan Pharmacy, owned by Henry C. Lawrence, and lived with his Uncle Caleb and Aunt "Hennie" (Henriette) Lilly. The job at the Good Samaritan allowed him to learn the fine points of being a pharmacist and chemist and the necessary skills to run a business. He remained there for five years before moving back to Greencastle.

Shortly after his return, he opened his own drugstore on the town square with a little financial assistance from his father. He was 24 years old.

Feeling confident of himself and his business, he married his childhood sweetheart, Emily Lemon, whose father was a merchant in the city. His life would change forever when the war began.

Answering the Union's call for soldiers, Lilly left both his bride and his treasured business and accepted a commission as a lieutenant in the 21st Indiana Volunteer Infantry. The Unit's name was changed to the First Heavy Artillery in February of 1863.

Instead of seeing offensive combat, the 21st Indiana was shipped to Baltimore as a defensive force to protect the local harbor, which

Eli Lilly, 21st Infantry

at that time was considered an important and likely target. After six months of frustrating inactivity, Second Lieutenant Eli Lilly resigned his commission on December 3, 1861 and returned home to Indiana.

Lilly may have resigned his commission, but he was not done with his desire to support the Union cause. He began to study artillery procedures and practices, memorizing tactics and artillery technique, and learning the theory of battlefield maneuvers and then began badgering Governor Morton for permission to form an artillery battery.

Impressed with Lilly's persistence and effort, Governor Morton appointed Lilly as Captain of the 18th Indiana Volunteer Light Artillery Battery in July of 1862. His orders were to recruit and lead the new unit.

His appointment by Morton was somewhat of a surprise to everyone since Lilly's only previous military experience, other than his time with the 21st Infantry, was being a member of a militia unit while working in Lafayette, Indiana.[43]

Within a month of his appointment, Lilly had recruited enough farmers, college students, friends, and foreigners to fill his artillery unit. In August of 1862, these men and boys reported to Camp Morton for artillery training.

Although the quick recruitment of the men was impressive, it caused serious logistical problems. While the new enlistees were ready to learn, there were no artillery weapons available to train them. The men, expecting an exciting and tough basic training, didn't enjoy sitting around with nothing to do. They eventually began complaining to Captain Lilly about the lack of drills and instruction. Lilly was also frustrated, and after much pleading and pulling whatever strings he could, the ordinance was finally delivered on September 1.

In a badly-timed twist of fate, the weapons arrived as Lilly received orders for the 18th Artillery to head to Kentucky and assist in repelling confederate General Braxton Bragg's invasion into the state. Lily's unit quickly assembled and headed south with no training and no clue as to how the weapons worked.

Fortunately, the untrained 18th Indiana did not have to participate in the skirmish. By the time they reached the site General Bragg had moved back across the Kentucky border and into Tennessee. Since Bragg was no longer a threat, Lilly's battery finally had time to train and conduct gunnery practice before being sent into action again. They would make Lieutenant Lilly proud when they next did battle.[44]

Chapter 5

The *Sultana*

While the war raged on, the King family continued their everyday family life. Katherine managed the home and cared for the children while John was working at a blacksmith shop. The month that the Kings' new baby, George, turned nine months old in February of 1863, John's hometown newspaper, the *Cincinnati Daily Commercial*, published an article about the maiden voyage of the newly built steamboat *Sultana*. The ship was scheduled for its first run on the Ohio River, heading northeast to Pittsburgh, Pennsylvania, with well-known boat builder Preston Lodwick as its owner and captain.

The new ship was said to be one of the largest and best business steamers ever constructed. At a cost of $64,000, she was equipped with four coal-burning boilers, measured two hundred and sixty feet long, and carried a pair of side-wheels with an eight-foot bucket capacity.

The steamboat business was a competitive one and plush furnishings, quality food, fine china, and other luxuries were the order of the day in the battle for business with an ever-growing number of competitors. The *Sultana* was no exception. She boasted a beautiful saloon with its own fully stocked ornate wooden bar, glass chandeliers, a secluded ladies section that was carpeted, oil paintings, and very comfortable staterooms.[45] Although the *Sultana* promoted its amenities for travelers, Lodwick planned on making a good portion of his profits hauling cargo.

The big day came on February 11, 1863. The *Sultana* was launched into the Ohio River and the fully loaded boat left the Cincinnati levee, making its way through the icy river. She was carrying six hundred tons of freight and, according to the *Daily Missouri Republican*, "A fair amount of passengers."

Three days later, Captain Lodwick proudly steered his showpiece up to the dock at Wheeling, West Virginia and quickly unloaded his ship's freight and passengers. As the ship prepared to move on toward Pittsburgh, the captain and his crew made a shocking discovery.

The height of the *Sultana*'s smokestacks would not clear the bridge that spanned the Ohio just north of Wheeling, which would make it impossible for them to make the last forty-mile leg of their scheduled trip to Pittsburgh. Lodwick was extremely embarrassed and irate over the predicament.

While he was pacing and fuming over this setback, the captain received another dose of bad news. A federal agent walked on board, without prior notification, and informed Lodwick that when the *Sultana* arrived back in Cincinnati the government would take control of his ship. The U.S. government had decided that it wanted to use the *Sultana* for shipping supplies and troops to aid in the war effort.

It's very likely that the *Sultana* was chosen because of her below-deck storage space and the extra-wide deck in front of the Pilothouse. Both of these allowed the ship to haul a larger-than-normal load. This was a terrible break for Lodwick and the *Sultana* on their maiden voyage but there was absolutely nothing he could do to change the government's decision.

In spite of this sudden bad turn of events the captain remained a resourceful and practical businessman. He took on a load of sugar and coffee and a few passengers in Wheeling and headed back to Cincinnati.

Six days later, the *Sultana* made her first war-time run to Louisville with a full load of military cargo. After a one-day layover, the *Sultana* returned to Cincinnati and Captain Lodwick's prized steamer began a constant round-trip route from Cincinnati to Wheeling.

This route lasted until May 5, when Lodwick was given orders to make his way down the Ohio River to the more dangerous waters of the Mississippi. Despite his concerns and fears, Captain Lodwick had no choice but to obey orders, cast off, and head down the Ohio. After a day-long trip the *Sultana* docked at Memphis. From there, she was ordered to St. Louis where the ship began to regularly travel up and down the big river, running all the way to New Orleans and back to St. Louis again. This was the original plan that Lodwick had for the *Sultana,* minus the war.

Although Union forces controlled nearly all of the Mississippi River, the Confederates took every opportunity to attack passing federal ships. On May 18, a little over a week after the *Sultana* began her trips up and down the river, she was heading south toward Columbia, Arkansas with four other ships.

In a surprise attack, all were fired on by ground-based Rebel artillery. The frantic Captain Lodwick quickly mobilized his crew and sped away, managing to escape without any damage to his ship.

After about ten weeks of traveling the dangerous Mississippi for the Union government the *Sultana* docked at St. Louis with a cargo of 186 horses and 63 mules. While there, Captain Lodwick learned that he would get some relief from his full-time government assignments.

He would continue with some military cargo shipments, but he would be free to take on commercial loads as well. This was great news for Lodwick, but he remained concerned. The river was still a dangerous place for any Yankee ship.[46]

Chapter 6

The War Comes to Indiana

The month after Lodwick was given his good news, an unexpected and alarming event took place in Indiana: Confederate General John Hunt Morgan initiated a plan to infiltrate the southern part of the state. His purpose was to determine what support, if any, he could get from Southern sympathizers during a raid into Indiana territory. Morgan eventually decided it was a worthy-if risky-mission and selected Captain Thomas H. Hines, an outstanding officer and a member in Company D of the General's Cavalry Regiment, to be the leader of his covert operation. When Hines briefed his men on the project, he told them that it would be a dangerous mission and that any man who did not wish to go could drop out; no one accepted the offer.

The first stop as the group headed north was Brownsville, Kentucky. They managed to steal Union uniforms, including shirts, trousers, and boots, from a local Union sutler, an authorized vendor of non-issue military supplies.

The next stop was Elizabethtown, Kentucky. While there, they robbed a train of enough Union currency to finance their mission. When they reached the Ohio River, Hines laid out the plan for his men. They would pose as Union soldiers and claim they were acting under orders from General Jeremiah T. Boyle to pursue deserters in the area known as the Indiana Grays.

Once the Rebel troops crossed the Ohio River, they rode

straight to Paoli, Indiana. They were eating dinner and wearing their Union clothing when a group of Indiana Home Guard entered the town and exposed the hoax. Hines and his men were able to escape and headed for French Lick. Shortly after reaching the city, they were again forced to run.

They were told that Union troops were approaching the town so, still dressed as Union soldiers, they moved on to Valeene, Indiana. By now, the men were hungry, but they were short on rations. Stopping at a nearby house the still disguised Reb's asked the occupants for dinner. The family refused.

The irate imposters burned their house down in response. It was a fatal mistake, as this action quickly made it clear to the locals in Valeene that these men were actually Confederates.

In a desperate move, Captain Hines hired a local man, Bryant Breeden, a laborer originally from Brandenberg, Kentucky, to lead them to a safe place. Why he chose Breeden is unknown, but Breeden turned out to be a Union supporter. He betrayed Hines by leading the group to Little Blue Island, a small landmass in the middle of the Ohio River near Leavenworth, Indiana. They were soon discovered, and a skirmish ensued. Three of Hines's men were killed.

Captain Hines managed to escape across the river with a few of his men. The rest of his band of imposters covered his escape. The men left behind eventually surrendered, and the Indiana Home Guard received high praise for their ability to rout the enemy in spite of their lack of combat experience.[47]

Chapter 7

Crown Hill Cemetery

Around that same time in Indianapolis the city was facing a minor crisis with the local cemetery. Greenlawn Cemetery, founded in 1821, was the main cemetery for Indianapolis and Marion County. It was located about seven blocks southwest of where Monument Circle stands today.

The city had been experiencing a population growth, and the small, cramped and poorly maintained burial grounds at Greenlawn Cemetery was now nearly full. Add to that the deaths of Indiana troops on battlefields and of Confederate prisoners being held at Camp Morton, and Indianapolis faced a severe shortage of places to bury its dead.

Early in 1863, the city and county officials reviewed the problem and determined that if an effort was made to correct the existing space problems within the cemetery there would be no room for future expansion of the city, so an alternative solution would be necessary. Governor Morton was informed of the effort and became involved in the project telling the group of officials that he would make a request for a national cemetery for Indianapolis. The effort moved forward and in the late summer of 1863, a committee was appointed to prepare for incorporation, hire a superintendent, and find the best location for the new cemetery grounds.

The committee, of course, consisted of some of the city's elite citizens: Mr. James M. Ray, a banker who earlier was the driving force behind the Indiana Institute for the Blind, was named president. Theodore P. Haughey, another bank president who would later be indicted by the federal government for misappropriating the funds of the Indianapolis National Bank, became secretary. A third banker, Stoughton A. Fletcher, Jr., the fifth child of Indianapolis's first banker, Calvin Fletcher, served as treasurer.

The committee commissioned John Chislet, Superintendent of Allegheny Cemetery in Pittsburgh, Pennsylvania, and three distinguished local men to search for the best possible site for the new cemetery within a six-mile radius of the city.

After visiting many suggested locations the four men made a visit to an area about three miles northwest of downtown Indianapolis that was known as Strawberry Hill. The area was part of a farm and nursery owned by Martin Williams, the same man who co-partnered with Gilbert Van Camp on the cold storage warehouse project and the opening of the Fruit House.

Strawberry Hill was the highest point of the lands surrounding the city and was often used by picnickers, especially when the annual ripe strawberries were free for the picking. When Mr. Chislet saw the area, he was immediately convinced that this should be the site of the new cemetery. He told the other men, "Buy those grounds at whatever price you have to pay."

While waiting for a reluctant Martin Williams to agree to a sale, the committee purchased forty acres of nearby land from retired merchant James Trueblood and another forty acres from Jonathon Wilson, a local farmer. By October of 1863, the agreement with Williams was completed and the first 236 acres of land had been purchased for a total of $51,000.

Fredrick Chislet, the son of John Chislet, and a landscape

architect himself, was named the first superintendent of Crown Hill Cemetery and moved his family into a small, already-existing cabin just south of the approach to "the Crown." His assignment was to design, build, and then care for the new cemetery.

On June 1, 1864, a dedication ceremony for the new funeral grounds was held to celebrate the long-awaited opening. Four hundred local citizens along with Governor Morton and members of the various committees attended the official opening.

The following day Lucy Ann Seaton became the first person buried at Crown Hill. The *Indianapolis Daily Journal* newspaper printed her obituary, which read,

June 2, 1864

DIED, of consumption in this city May 26,

Mrs. Lucy Ann Seaton,

Of Paducah, Kentucky.

She was born in Virginia, at Halifax, in 1830 and was at the time of her death 33 years, 7 months and 10 days of age. She was the friend of the poor and needy, a humble member of the M. E. Church, and experienced religion at a very early age, she truly loved her Jesus. Her loss is deeply deplored by her friends.

She was an excellent pattern, both as a kind wife and mother and a useful mentor to society. The funeral will take place today at 10 a.m., June 2nd. She will be buried at Crown Hill Cemetery and as this is the first internment in this place, as many as can should go out. The funeral will start from Matthew Long's Undertaker at precisely 10 a.m.

That same day, the paper ran a brief article about her burial, saying,

The first burial in Crown Hill Cemetery will take place today. The husband of the deceased is a gentleman of high standing and he is a stranger in the city. We hope his invitation to the public to join in the funeral ceremony will be accepted by a goodly number.

The heartbreaking death of Lucy was compounded when just four months later, her daughter Laura, age four, was buried beside her mother. Captain Seaton and his ten-year-old son were left to carry on as the last remaining members of their small family.

The Seatons led a nomadic life. Captain John Seaton was born in Mauchline, Ayrshire, Scotland in 1826. His family moved to the United States in 1828 and made their home in New York before moving to Battle Creek, Michigan and then west to Peoria, Illinois. In 1850, John's father, John Seaton, Sr., was working as a brick mason while John himself worked at a grocery.

In 1854, young John was living in Fayette, Tennessee when he met Lucy A. Hart, one of eleven children, born in Virginia to Elijah and Lucy (Douglas) Hart. On November 17, 1854, John and Lucy were married. Within a year, Lucy gave birth to their first child, John H. Seaton.

In April of 1860, Lucy gave birth to a second child, Laura, in the state of Illinois. Two months later, the Seatons were living in Hickman, Kentucky—located in the furthest southwest corner of the state—where John was a teacher in the local school.

In January of that same year, the town of Hickman suffered a disastrous fire that destroyed half of the town. Newspaper accounts stated, "All the buildings on Front Street, which contained the principal business houses, were laid in ashes."

Hickman was a Confederate hotbed at the time and as the threat of cessation and war increased, the Seatons moved back to Illinois.

On August 31, 1861, John volunteered to serve in the 22nd Illinois Infantry and was assigned to Company B with the immediate rank of captain. His tenure was short-lived.

Nine months after enlisting, on May 30, 1862, Captain Seaton resigned his commission. Military records state that, "Tenders resignation—ill health of wife renders presence necessary at home. Paid to May 1, 1862. No property onhand except guns and equipments of Company which he is ready to turn over at any time."

Why the Seatons were in Indianapolis at the time of the deaths of Lucy and her daughter is unknown.

After Lucy and Laura's burial, father and son moved to a Cynthiana, Kentucky farm that was owned by the Seaton family, where Captain Seaton remarried another Lucy—a widow named Lucy M. McAfee—whose father was a prominent Presbyterian bishop in Paducah, Kentucky. The Seatons raised shorthorn cattle and Poland China hogs on this farm.

John L. Seaton died December 28, 1886 and was buried in Battle Grove Cemetery in Cynthiana, Kentucky. His son, John H., continued on with the family business.[48]

The same month the Crown Hill Project was initiated, the *Sultana* left Helena, Arkansas on a late July run carrying another load of cargo and three high-ranking Union generals. The boat headed south, passing Memphis, and had gone about forty-five miles when she was attacked by a Confederate unit. The Reb's rapid fire badly damaged the upper works of the ship before the *Sultana* could get away.

Four days later as the steamer was moving north toward St. Louis and carrying 672 bales of prized cotton, she was attacked again.

Fortunately, she managed to escape with no serious harm to the ship or the crew.[49]

Chapter 8

Indiana Troops at Gettysburg

While the *Sultana* was making her cargo and troop runs up and down the Mississippi, two major events occurred in the month of July 1863 that raised deep concern among the citizens of Indiana and throughout the nation.

Rebel General Robert E. Lee's Army of Northern Virginia moved across the southern border of Pennsylvania and into Union territory on the first day of July in 1863. His intent was to re-supply his troops for a deeper invasion into the North, possibly into Philadelphia, Baltimore, or Washington.

Having already won several battles against Union forces, it was Lee's belief that his army could not lose a battle against the Northern troops. He was so convinced that he was willing to gamble everything on the fact that he could defeat the Union forces in the North and hopefully weaken and destroy a large portion of the northern army in the process. His goal was to turn the tide of the war in favor of the South. He would be doing battle in Pennsylvania against the Union forces of Major General George G. Meade, whom he knew could have nearly 97,000 troops under his command in three days' time.

Undaunted, General Lee moved forward with an eventual 75,000 troops under his command. On July 1, 1863, Lee initiated the first battle in this campaign by attacking General John Buford's Union Cavalry division on McPherson Ridge. The site was about a mile west of the city of Gettysburg, Pennsylvania, and the confrontation on that ridge was the beginning of one of the bloodiest battles in American history.[50]

Union General John Buford had two troops of dismounted cavalry posted on McPherson Ridge the day of Lee's attack; they were watching the roads heading into town. During the watch, Buford spotted a long line of Rebel troops marching toward his position. The line was stretched out at an angle reaching from the northeast to the southwest. He could see that the Reb's were coming and that they were ready for a battle.

With only a few hundred men at his disposal, Buford knew he was vastly outnumbered. Although his troops had the advantages of high ground and better weapons, the overwhelming number of enemy soldiers put him at a huge disadvantage. He immediately dispatched riders to request help from nearby units.

The Union troops fought well throughout the day and Buford's cavalry units held the Rebs at bay until the Union First and Eleventh Corps arrived. The First Corps was an outstanding Unit and although they had to retreat at some point during this skirmish, they ultimately stopped the charging enemy troops.[51]

Over the next two days additional troops for both armies arrived, including several Indiana units. The 3rd Indiana Cavalry, 7th Indiana Infantry, 14th Indiana Infantry, 20th Indiana Infantry, and 27th Indiana Infantry all took part in what was to become the deadliest battle of the war.

On the morning of July 2, believing that the Confederates he was facing were in a vulnerable position, Union Colonel Silas Colgrove, a former member of the Indiana House of Representatives from Winchester, Indiana, ordered the 27th Indiana into a charge against the Rebel forces.

As soon as the charge began, they were hit with a relentless barrage of Southern lead. The Hoosiers of the 27th only made it halfway across the open field before retreating. In the process, they lost nearly a third of their men. It was a tremendous sacrifice with nothing to show for their heroic and misguided effort.[52]

During the second day of the battle, Terre Haute enlistee Private Oliver P. Rood of Company B, 20th Indiana Infantry was with his unit which was positioned almost due south of the city of Gettysburg on the property of local farmer John Rose. Rood's Indiana unit found themselves in a battle with several Confederate brigades, including General Robert F. Hoke's 21st North Carolina Infantry.

The skirmish between the 20th Indiana and the 21st North Carolina began in Rose's woods and soon moved into his adjacent wheat field where the fighting was extraordinarily intense and violent. By the end of the day, Farmer Rose's wheat crop would be trampled to the ground and soaked with blood.

The next day, the fighting moved east to Cemetery Ridge, where the Indiana troops were forced to defend against a charge from Rebel Major General George Edward Pickett, who was making a last-ditch, futile effort to win the battle. During that charge, the Union troops fought ferociously to drive back the charging Rebs. After an intense and brutal fight, they were able to force the Southern troops to retreat.

As the 21st North Carolina Infantry fled the Union onslaught, Private Rood managed to capture the flag of the retreating North Carolina troops.

The battle flags of both sides had become powerful military symbols and great significance was placed on the capture of an enemy flag. For his action, Rood was later awarded the Congressional Medal of Honor. He was the only Indiana soldier to receive the award for heroism at Gettysburg. The award ceremony took place right on the battlefield.

After three short days of exchanged gunfire, heavy shelling, and hand-to-hand combat, the battle that nearly changed the outcome of the war was over. This major confrontation between the two armies saw more men fighting and dying on North American soil than any battle before or after the Civil War.

Injury and death in the Civil War were many and merciless: Cannon balls, grapeshot, canister, musket balls, bayonets, sabers, clubbing, or hand-to-hand combat inflicting injury or death. Men were decapitated, cut in two, blown apart, shot, bashed in the face or skull, disemboweled, burned, dragged, or drowned. Many men died agonizing deaths after various battles, lying injured on the field for hours or days and left to die among the already dead.

When the battle of Gettysburg was over, the North had finally won the battle, but at a costly and appalling loss of life on both sides. Lee began his southern retreat into Virginia on the afternoon of July 4, leaving behind the 2,400 traumatized residents of the small town of Gettysburg and over 51,000 Union and Rebel casualties. Two of the survivors of the battle were Major General Abner Doubleday and Brigadier General George Armstrong Custer.[53]

The Indiana contingent at Gettysburg included five infantry and elements of two cavalry regiments. The 7th, 14th, 19th, 20th, and 27th Infantry and portions of the 1st Indiana Volunteer Cavalry and the 3rd Indiana Cavalry accounted for over 2,200 Hoosiers at the battle of Gettysburg. Five hundred and fifty-two of those became casualties.[54]

Just four days after the brutal battle of Gettysburg, the war moved a lot closer to home for the King family. Despite orders to stay south of the Ohio river, Brigadier General John Morgan led his Rebel troops across the river from Kentucky and into the town of Mauckport, Indiana on July 8, 1863, where they camped overnight.

The next day, Morgan's 2,500 troops did battle with about 400 hastily assembled Militiamen from the Home Guard 6th Indiana Legion Regiment near Corydon, Indiana.

Nearly all 400 of the Indiana troops were captured. The Reb's moved on from Corydon and through the towns of Lexington, Vernon, North Vernon, Bryantsburg, Versailles, and Osgood.

In each city, the Reb's looted businesses, robbed the townspeople, and destroyed bridges, railroads, and government stores as they rampaged through southern Indiana. Morgan eventually released the captured Hoosier guardsmen from Corydon before moving east into Ohio.

Although raids had previously been made in Indiana by the Rebs, namely at Newburgh and Paoli, the "Battle of Corydon", as it was named, was the only officially recognized battle in the Civil War that was fought on Indiana soil.[55]

The second major event in early July occurred when Eli Lilly's 18th Indiana Artillery made two major contributions to the Union effort in Tennessee. The 18th had been assigned to Colonel John T. Wilder's Mounted Brigade, which led to Lilly's troops participating in Major General William S. Rosecrans's Army of the Cumberland Tennessee Campaign. The 18th had become the brigade's artillery support.

When Rosecrans was ordered into action against General Braxton Bragg in Middle Tennessee, it gave Lilly and his men a second chance at a battle and an opportunity to showcase their recent training. Their first real action took place as the Union troops ultimately engaged Bragg at Hoover's Gap, Tennessee.

On their arrival they saw the Confederate forces were well positioned, but Wilder's brigade made a brutal attack, pushing the Rebs out of position. With the enemy now in range, Lilly's battery cut loose with impressive and effective fire, sending the Confederates into full retreat and earning high praise from the general.

A second showing of Lilly's 18th's artillery skills took place when Wilder's troops reached the Tennessee River opposite Chattanooga and the general ordered Lilly's 18th Indiana to begin shelling the town. The volley of shells caught many soldiers and civilians in church, observing a day of prayer and fasting.

The bombardment sank two steamers that were docked at the landing and generally created panic and chaos among the local residents and the Rebel troops. When Bragg's men recovered, Confederate Captain William Fowler's Alabama battery began returning fire and the battle was on.

Lilly's 18th responded by firing a volley of long-range canister and percussion shells. During the exchange of fire, a bizarre incident took place. One of the Rebels' shells landed near Lilly's Number Two gun, ricocheting and hitting the corner of a log house before bouncing back among Lilly's men. The fuse of the shell was still burning when seventeen-year-old Private Sidney Speed from Crawfordsville, Indiana quickly ran over, picked up the live shell, and threw it over the house where it exploded harmlessly. Following the battle, a very shocked and impressed Colonel Lilly noted in his records that he had given Private Speed a citation of gallantry. The 18th Indiana brigade would eventually become the most renowned fighting unit in the Army of the Cumberland and was given the name "The "Lightning Brigade." [56]

Henry Campbell was only sixteen years old when he enlisted in Captain Lilly's 18th Indiana Artillery. He had been refused enlistment before but Lilly accepted the young clerk from Crawfordsville as the battery's bugler, which was a huge responsibility for anyone regardless of age. After a few days of drill, Henry made a brief trip home for a visit. When he returned to his unit, he began having second thoughts. In his next letter to his family in Crawfordsville, where his father was a merchant, he wrote, "Left home forever. Never expected to live through the hardships."

The following August, a surgeon who was assigned to examine Lilly's troops said he considered Henry too young for military service. Again, Lilly stepped in and argued that it was "essential to the interests of the service" that the young man be kept as the company bugler. Henry stayed and after a year and a half with the 18th Henry Campbell was given a commission as second lieutenant in the 101st US Colored Infantry. [57]

Chapter 9

Lincoln at Gettysburg

In November of 1863, President Abraham Lincoln left Washington for a train trip to Gettysburg. He had been asked to "say a few remarks" at the site of the now-revered battlefield. Lincoln, although still upset with General George G. Meade for not following and finishing off Lee's army, wanted to honor the Union troops and made the six-hour trip, arriving on November 18, 1863.

Lincoln awoke the next morning feeling ill and looking out at a rainy and fog-filled sky. After learning that this speech had become a major event and that thousands of people were already waiting for him, he felt obligated to speak even though he was ill.

Some of the locals were primed to take advantage of the situation. Tables were set up near the ceremony site and the entrepreneurs were ready to make money. Among items for sale were cookies, lemonade, and Gettysburg souvenirs. Soldier's buttons, canteens, and dead wildflowers straight from the battlefield were sold to the large and growing crowd of excited citizens.

The president arrived in a new suit and a black stovepipe hat, suffering from a fever. Former US Senator Edward Everett spoke first, rambling on for two hours and detailing each day of the event and each battle for the rain-soaked crowd. Lincoln spoke for two minutes, giving one of the most famous and enduring speeches in our nation's history. As he headed back to Washington, he laid across his seat on the train with a wet towel over his eyes and forehead, believing his speech had been a total failure. It was later determined that the President had a mild case of Smallpox.[58]

Chapter 10

A Life Altering Decision

The ongoing war and its consequences were on the minds of many concerned Hoosiers'. The disturbing news and events that filled the Indiana newspapers became the main subject of conversation throughout the state of Indiana. The recent news and the current status of the war may very well have helped John King make his decision; he chose this time to finally make a commitment and, despite his family obligations at home, enlisted on December 14, 1863 in Indianapolis, Indiana for a three-year hitch.

His enlistment papers show that he was enrolled as Joseph H. King, also born as John H. King, that his age was thirty-two, that he was five feet, five inches tall, and had a light complexion, blue eyes, and sandy hair.[59] He was assigned to a newly-formed unit, Company F of the 9th Indiana Cavalry, 121st Regiment, under Colonel George W. Jackson.[60]

The second in command was Major Eli Lilly. Lilly's term

9th Indiana Cavalry: Col. George W. Jackson & Major. Eli Lilly

Private John H. King

with the 18th Artillery had been completed and he was unhappy with the command to which his unit had been assigned. Rather than stay with his original unit, he returned to Indianapolis to accept an upgrade in rank and assist Colonel Jackson with recruiting and training.[61]

Originally, the local military training facilities were at Camp Morton in Indianapolis, which was named after current Governor Oliver P. Morton. The camp was located on land that had previously been the Indiana state fairgrounds, but had been requisitioned by Governor Morton and his newly appointed adjutant general, Lew Wallace.

General Wallace was born and educated in Brookville, Indiana, where Gilbert Van Camp was born and was just a few miles from Metamora, where Katherine and Hester had grown up. His father, David Wallace, was the governor of the state of Indiana from 1837 to 1840.

Through the efforts of the governor and General Wallace, Camp Morton opened on April 17, 1861. Although the fort was not quite ready, new recruits arrived and training began. After preliminary efforts at training they soon realized that the camp was not suitable for anything beyond basic drills due to the vast number of oak and walnut trees and all of the old state fair buildings, some of which were now in use as offices, barracks, and mess halls.

Better natural features and more open space were needed,

so in 1862 a new facility, Camp Murray, was built to handle the recruitment and training of enlistees and volunteers. Camp Murray was located between the canal and Fall Creek near present-day 15th and Missouri Streets. The name was later changed to Camp Carrington, for General Henry B. Carrington who served as colonel and brigadier general in the Union Army. It was one of the largest of the twenty-four camps established in the Indianapolis area during the war.

This turned out to be not only a necessary move but a fortunate one. In February of 1862, Camp Morton became a northern prison camp for Confederate troops.

Camp Carrington is where John H. King received his training.[62]

He may have thought his experience as a blacksmith would land him a similar job when he enlisted, but frontline troops were considered essential. They instead chose to train him to fight on horseback as part of the Indiana cavalry. Although John was familiar with horses and blacksmithing, he was not a trained horseman, a soldier, or a cavalryman. In his early training, he had to learn the basic protocol of the military, such as saluting, rank, marching, and proper dress, and as a mounted trooper was taught the principles of dismounted drill, mounted drill, and facing movements.

He was trained to mount a horse from either side, how to pack his saddle, and how to use and care for his personal equipment. This was the easy part. When he was provided a horse of his own, the training became more difficult. Riding a horse in the middle of a skirmish required not only skill with both rifle and saber, but stamina, as well. John and his fellow recruits learned that commands during battle were given by both voice and bugle and each bugle call meant something different. Cavalry manuals listed as many as thirty-eight separate calls.

They included:

1. The General
2. Boots and Saddles
3. To Horse
4. The Assembly
5. To Arms
6. To the Standard
7. The March
8. The Charge
9. The Rally
10. Reveille
11. Stable Call
12. Watering Call
13. Breakfast Call
14. Assembly of the Guard
15. Orders for Orderly Sergeants
16. Assembly of the Trumpeters
17. Retreat
18. Fatigue Call
19. Dinner call
20. Distributions
21. Drill Call
22. Officers Call
23. The recall
24. Sick Call
25. Tattoo (Prepare for bed/secure post)
26. To Extinguish Lights

A second group rounded out the thirty-eight separate calls.

1. Forward
2. Halt
3. To the left
4. To the right
5. The about
6. Change direction to the right
7. Change direction to the left
8. Trot
9. Gallop
10. Commence firing
11. Cease fire
12. Charge as foragers[63]

The ability to recognize the proper call was crucial. In battle, a misunderstood call could bring complete chaos and result in the death of your fellow troops. The first and foremost task of the cavalry recruit however was to learn how to care for his horse. John had to quickly learn the ways of and signals from his horse, which by now had also learned the bugle sounds.

Whether in battle or just training, the horses could not perform well without adequate food, water, and rest, so much of John's training time revolved around learning the limitations and requirements of his horse. He was taught early on that his horse was the key to his performance and, more importantly, his survival.[64]

Around the first of January in 1864, while John was training at Camp Carrington the *Sultana* had finally begun her full-time commercial trade business from her home port of St. Louis, which had been established during her military service. Preston Lodwick was still the owner and captain of the ship.

By March of that same year, the *Sultana* had created a nice return on Lodwick's investment. The *Sultana*'s profit was now nearly double the cost of her construction. Also by that March, at age sixty-four, Lodwick had a new-found love interest. He began looking for a buyer for his ship.

Lodwick had recently begun spending more time with his new fiancé and was now relinquishing control of the *Sultana* to Captain J. Cass Mason, a former captain of the *Belle Memphis,* which ran the same basic route as the *Sultana.* Mason was anxious to own his own boat and with the help of two St. Louis businessmen he bought the *Sultana* from Lodwick for $90,000. Mason was now not only the Captain but had a three-eighths ownership. The new partners took control and the *Sultana* once again took to the Mississippi in anticipation of a profitable venture.[65]

Chapter 11

Skirmishes of the 9th Indiana Cavalry

At the end of April 1864 John King finished his boot camp training and had learned all the army could teach him about the cavalry. However, **nothing** in his training could have prepared him for what he would face in the months and years to come.

The 121st Regiment remained in the state under drill until the 3rd of May, 1864 when John and his fellow troops left Indiana by rail on the first leg of a long trip to Nashville, Tennessee.[66] That same day, Indiana Governor Oliver P. Morton was taking some heat from the *Indianapolis Daily Evening Gazette*. President Lincoln had just issued a call for a 100-day enlistment campaign to supply a brief increase in the number of troops available to the north.

Taking exception to Governor Morton's response, the paper published an article on the front page titled "The Injustice to Indiana." The editors stated,

"Ohio has nearly double the population of Indiana and Illinois numbers much more, at least twenty five or thirty percent. Indiana's proportion of the eighty five thousand 'hundred's day men' offered to Mr. Lincoln by the Governor's of Ohio, Illinois, Indiana, Iowa and Wisconsin would be about thirteen thousand. Notwithstanding this difference in the population Governor Morton offered to put Indiana upon a par with Ohio, and Illinois. To say nothing about

placing this burden upon the Western States when New England and the Eastern States have not even filled their quotas, and our state is in excess of all the demands made upon her. Governor Morton pledges Indiana, without the knowledge or concept of her citizens however, for just as many militia or 'hundred day men' as did the governors of Ohio and Illinois.

Why should Indiana be thus burdened? Was Governor Morton overreached by Governors Brough and Yates, or was he willing, as the representative of Indiana, to place this burden upon her people to advance his personal interests?" [67]

The governor's wife also made the paper that same day in the "City Section." A small item gave notice of her attempt to help in the war effort saying, "The ladies of the Third Ward will meet on Wednesday May 4, at two o'clock, p.m. and on every succeeding Wednesday afternoon during the month of May at the house of Mrs. Joseph Curson˙, NO. 218 North Illinois Street, to sew and knit for the soldiers. It is very desirable that we should have a good supply ready for any emergency.

By Order of Mrs. O.P Morton, President." [68]

While the bickering and knitting continued in Indy, John and his fellow recruits of the 9th Indiana Cavalry and their available horses were headed to Lawrenceburg, Indiana.

Because of the shortage of horses, a portion of the men were listed as "dismounted." Some of the other troops purchased their own horses with help from a partial stipend from a government allowance. John King was among the men who were unable to purchase a horse.

On May 4, the 9th Indiana troops arrived in Lawrenceburg, Indiana at 2 a.m. Two hours later, they were put on board a riverboat and headed to Louisville. They arrived in the late afternoon of that same day, marched south for two hours, and made camp for the night.[69]

They were up and on the move at 7:00 a.m. the next day. The unit arrived at their designated campsite just outside of Nashville in good time, and they were not alone. The area was a base camp for five Indiana Cavalry units. The other four Indiana Cavalry units present were the 10th, with men from Columbus, Vincennes, Terre Haute, New Albany, and Indianapolis; the 11th, which had recruits from Lafayette, Kokomo, and Indianapolis; the 12th, which was staffed with men from Kendallville and Michigan City; and the 13th Cavalry, which, although organized in Indianapolis, included men from Kokomo and New Albany. Quite an impressive group of Indiana troops committed to the Union.

The area around the camp was thick with underbrush and nestled against a large patch of woods. The men soon discovered what they called a "large hill" just behind the woods. Having come from the farm lands of Indiana, they were all duly impressed when they could stand on the top of the "hill" and see for miles.

Eighteen-year-old Private William Wheeler of the 9th Indiana Cavalry, Company D, was originally from Ohio but later lived in Richmond, Indiana and Dublin, Indiana. He said he was able to look from his tent opening and see "a sort of mountain with hills and hollers between here and there." [70]

Two days later, Private Wheeler took advantage of his new surroundings and made his way to the nearby Tennessee River, going for a swim. Although thoroughly enjoying the dip and feeling refreshed he noted, "The flies are terrible bad here!" [71] Private Wheeler would later found an organization for the homeless, poor, and needy in Indianapolis named Wheeler Mission.

As John King settled into his active-duty army life, the days were long and hard. Each day, he faced constant drilling in the Manual of Arms, he had to eat hard bread and salted meat for meals, and suffered the boredom of Army life while sleeping in a tent on the hard-packed Tennessee dirt.

General John Franklin Miller was now in command of the city of Nashville, Tennessee and the garrison of troops in the area.

Born in South Bend, Indiana, he joined the Union Army at the outbreak of the Civil War and was commissioned Colonel of the 29th Indiana Infantry. Miller had just returned to duty following an eleven-month medical leave. He had been shot in the left eye by an Enfield rifle in a battle at Murfreesboro, Tennessee.

Prior to taking command at Nashville, he was promoted to brigadier general and, for his services at the battle of Nashville, he was made a brevetted major general. Despite the loss of his sight in one eye and the pain from the bullet wedged against his brain, he continued to lead. He did not have the bullet removed until twelve years later. Following the war, he became a distinguished US senator from the state of California.[72]

After a short stay under Miller's command, the troops were ordered to move out to Bridgeport, Alabama and set up their camp. By noon on May 23, the men had broken camp, packed up and were ready to head southeast. John King and his fellow troopers began a 100-mile march in pouring rain.

The men moved out around 11:00 p.m. By midnight, the totally drenched men felt like they had been marching for hours in enemy territory. During the trek, John and the other men received a little unexpected boost to their morale when they spotted a rare site, two homes displaying white flags indicating either their neutrality or their support for the northern troops.[73]

Despite the heavy rainstorm, the troops made excellent time, arriving in the city just as the sun was coming up. Once again, Private King joined his fellow troops as they cleared the area, pitched tents, and set up the hospital and cooking areas. Then once again grudgingly began the same daily grind of drill, eat, and sleep.

On May 27, the troops received orders to move out. The destination was Pulaski, Tennessee. At 9:00 a.m. the next morning, the men and horses were loaded on a train and began the seventy-three mile trek northwest to Pulaski, which was about twenty miles north of the Alabama border.[74]

The 9th arrived in the city on May 29 with a promise of horses for the dismounted men, but they soon learned that there were not enough horses to mount all the troops in the area. The horse shortage became so bad that at one point General John Starkweather, commander of the post at Pulaski, had 2,212 cavalrymen on hand and only 536 horses. Although a few additional horses arrived, the men still outnumbered the horses.[75]

After some negotiation among the officers of the various units, the 9th Indiana was given seventy percent of the available horses, but companies D, E, and—much to John King's dismay-Company F were left without horses and relegated to blockhouse guard duty. Blockhouse's were fortified log structures with open ports through which the men could direct their gunfire. Those three companies were also assigned to guard the local railroad.[76]

When the men were issued rifles, four men from Company D refused to take what they considered inferior weapons and were put under arrest.[77]

Some of the men from these units had their horses taken from them and given to other companies, causing a near-mutiny. The remaining men of the 9th Indiana, who were all mounted, were paired with the 3rd Tennessee Union Cavalry and assigned to scout the nearby areas of Tennessee and Alabama and engage the enemy at every opportunity. The Confederates had been busy tearing up bridges and railroads.

On September 25, 1864, word of a Rebel plot for an attack at Elk River and the Sulphur Branch Trestle reached brigade commander General John Starkweather. He quickly ordered the 10th Indiana to proceed to Elk River Bridge and assigned Major Eli Lilly and 128 men of the 9th Indiana to accompany them. When they arrived at the bridge, there was no activity and no sign of any Rebel troops.

The 10th Indiana remained at Elk River while Lilly and the 9th headed toward a Fort Henderson, a small nearby Garrison constructed to guard the Trestle.

The Trestle was a wooden bridge spanning a 70 foot ravine. It was 400 feet in length and one of the most important points between Nashville and Decatur on the Alabama and Tennessee railroad.

Shortly after Lilly and his troops arrived, he led his unit south on a reconnaissance toward the city of Athens. Soon after the troops began their search, they spotted a group of Confederates who were in a position to warn against an enemy advance. As the two groups met, they immediately engaged in a skirmish.

During the battle, Lilly spotted the troops of General Nathan B. Forrest moving toward them. He was shocked to see a line of Confederate cavalry that was over a mile long. Lilly hurriedly ordered a messenger to return to the fort and inform Colonel William H. Lathrop, Union commander of the 110th and 111th Alabama US Colored Infantry, of the grave news.

When Lilly was able to break free from the skirmish, he and his men returned to the fort and met with Lathrop who had hurriedly designed a plan of defense. The fort was a crude and simple design made up of earthen embankments and fortified with two wooden blockhouses. It was built at the bottom of a steep ravine with sheer rock walls on three sides and overlooked an open clearing to the south. Any approaching enemy from that direction would be exposed in an open field to take fire.[78]

The troops at the fort consisted of the 3rd Tennessee Cavalry, Lathrop's own 110th Alabama unit, the 111th Alabama Infantry, and Lilly's returning 9th Indiana Cavalry troops. Lathrop distributed the men along the northern, western, and southwestern walls and prepared for battle. It wasn't long before Forrest and his massive army of 10,000 troops arrived and the one-sided fight began.

Corporal J. H. Brown and 10 other men from Lilly's unit had been assigned to stay outside of the fort and guard the horses. Corporal Brown later described the start of the Rebel shelling: "We remained with the horses until a cannon ball or slug or something of the kind. Anyhow, it was something from a Rebel gun landed about 15 feet from us. It tore a hole in the ground large enough to bury a small-sized cow and threw dirt all over us.

"We then thought it was time to desert the horses and let them take care of themselves and climb the hill and get into the fort as soon as we could, conveniently, without hurting ourselves, and up the hill we went and when we arrived at the entrance to the fort we asked where the 9th Indiana was stationed. We were told they were on the opposite side of the fort, so we had to go through the center of the fort to get where our boys were stationed. That was the most dangerous trip I ever experienced in my life.

"There were a lot of barracks in the fort and the Rebel cannon were playing on them and knocking them all to pieces and throwing the loose boards in every direction. It made the hair raise on our heads as we went dodging through the barracks among the flying boards, shells, and cannon ball, but we finally got to our men safely." [79]

As soon as the shelling began, Colonel Lathrop was killed and Colonel John B. Minnis of the 3rd Tennessee Cavalry took command. Minutes later, Minnis was knocked unconscious by a piece of shell. Within just a few short minutes, the two top officers of the fort were out of action, and Major Lilly became the ranking officer in charge.

The Union troops were giving it their all, but they had only two twelve-pound artillery pieces while Forrest had eight cannons. Even though the Yanks had the advantage of a fortified position, they were heavily outgunned and outnumbered.

To make matters worse, the placement of the fort at the bottom of the ravines allowed the Confederate artillery and sharpshooters to fire down on the Union troops from the higher ground surrounding the fort.

Forrest's artillery cut loose. Nearly 800 rounds aimed at the fort were fired in a little more than 2 hours. The Union troops tried to take cover in the wooden buildings, but the incessant artillery barrage either destroyed the structures or set them afire.[80] As the fort and men were falling around him, Major Lilly looked to the north and saw a heavy line of the enemy coming across open ground. To sound a warning he ordered a messenger to warn the officer in command of the colored troops and tell him to instruct his men cooly and firmly to meet the impending assault from the advancing Rebs head-on. The messenger was killed before he was out of sight. Lilly selected a second messenger, but he was also killed.

Lieutenant Hiram Jones of the 111th, Company M stepped up and volunteered to take the message. He also failed. He was wounded while zigzagging through the sniper fire and exploding shells that were raining down on the interior of the fort.

In desperation, Major Lilly took it upon himself to race across the bloody and body-strewn battlefield to deliver the message. He made it safely. One of Lilly's men, Corporal J.A. Brown, later said, "Major Lilly was a hustler! He was one of the bravest officers that ever went to the front."[81]

Despite a courageous attempt, the out-manned, out-gunned Union troops surrendered the following day when they realized they were nearly out of ammunition. Even though the Yanks were heavily outnumbered the battle lasted six hours. Lilly and the other units lost 96 men, but Forrest's troops saw 200 killed and 1,100 wounded. An amazing statistic considering the lopsided number of men and weapons.[82]

Nearly all of the Union defenders were captured. Major Lilly, Colonel Minnis (who had recovered) and the other officers were sent to the Confederate prison in Enterprise, Mississippi. The captured enlisted men were sent by train to the prison at Cahaba, Alabama.

The 110th and 111th colored troops were sent to Mobile, Alabama and put to work in the salt mines.[83]

In early November, following Lilly's surrender at Sulphur Trestle, John King was finally issued a horse and relieved of guard duty. Companies F, E, and D all received fresh horses and rejoined their mounted comrades in Pulaski, where they were waiting for equipment and their orders. On November 25, John King was issued a Maynard carbine and a saber.

The .50-caliber Maynard measured nearly 58 inches long and

weighed about six pounds, which was considerably lighter than other common carbines. Although some of the men complained of the excessive recoil, due to the gun's light weight, it was easy

Maynard Rifle Second Issue

Maynard Rifle Second Issue C.U.

9th Indiana Cavalry Saber

to use on horseback, was impressively accurate, and, like most cavalry rifles, could be attached to the trooper's saddle with a sling hook.[84]

Two days after receiving their weapons, John and the other men of the 9th started a five-mile march on the Franklin Pike through the drizzling rain and mud, stopping just south of Nashville to set up camp for the night.

The next day, November 28, they continued their march toward Franklin, Tennessee. The road was littered with contraband and refugees of all shapes and sizes and the displaced citizens from the area were a sorry sight. Some women were walking and carrying a child astride their shoulders. Sickly, broken-down mules were sometimes carrying two or three people. The Union troops were left to wonder where these people came from and where they were going.[85]

On the night of November 29, 1864, the 9th Indiana Cavalry was ordered to march across the Tribune Pike and repel a reported flanking movement by the Rebs. The anticipated action was a bust. The unit was unable to find any sign of enemy troops. The next morning, the men resumed their daily grind of waiting and watching, able to hear the sounds of muskets and the zip of a stray bullet throughout the morning but there was no confrontation or action.

Later that day, the sound of battle grew nearer and nearer. John and his fellow cavalrymen were ordered into line with drawn sabers. Suddenly, the sounds of musketry began to move further away. The anticipation came to nothing, a nerve wracking and stressful time for the troops. Some of the men believed that the expectation of battle might be more nerve-wracking than the actual fighting.

That evening, the 9th began a 20 mile march over the roughest terrain they had ever seen. The horses and the men fell to the ground several times as they tripped on rocks and fell into ditches. They finally stopped near the city of Triune, just southeast of Franklin, Tennessee, where they were fed. The horses were left saddled to save time before continuing their trek to Franklin. Fourteen miles away, a major and devastating incident was beginning to take shape around Spring Hill and Franklin, Tennessee.[86]

One of the ultimate leadership gaffes of the Confederate Army of Tennessee was made by the renowned General John B. Hood at Spring Hill and Franklin, Tennessee. He and his command allowed the escape of Major General John Schofield's army at Spring Hill on November 29, 1864.

Hood had ordered one of his divisions to Spring Hill in advance to contain the Union position north of Duck Creek. A Union defensive line made up of soldiers in Schofield's army was covering the approaches to that city and protecting a wagon train, the reserve artillery, and the local railroad.

When Hood's troops arrived, they were met with stiff resistance by Schofield's well-positioned troops. The Rebs were forced to change their plan of attack. When additional troops sent by Hood arrived the Rebel Army outnumbered Schofield's Union division, but an assault was never launched against the now-overmatched Yanks.

Confusing orders came from Hood's headquarters, often countermanding each other, and the assault with the additional troops never took place.

Instead, Hood ordered his men to set up camp for the night.

With the Rebel troops inactive and asleep on the night of April 29, 1864, the Union troops were able to slip by the exhausted, underfed, ragged Southerners.

Hood slept through the incident. He was taking pain killers and possibly drinking alcohol to lessen his chronic pain. General Hood was actually a physical wreck. He recently had fallen from his horse, he had a withered left arm and was missing his right leg from a previous battle. When Hood and his battle-weary army of Tennessee awoke the next morning, they discovered that the Yankees had slipped by them and were well on their way to Franklin.

After Schofield arrived in Franklin, he surveyed the terrain and the city and quickly decided to have his Union troops dig in and make a stand. He knew Hood would be arriving shortly.

When General Hood did arrive, he was still fuming about the fact that his subordinates had allowed Schofield's troops to escape during the previous night. After surveying the Union fortification, he decided to launch a frontal attack against the Union position, even though the Yanks had dug in and were waiting for a charge.

His rage still simmering, and before his artillery and one of his infantry companies were in place, he ordered a charge of his entire infantry against the entrenched and waiting Union soldiers. Holding their fire until the Rebs were nearly in front of them, Schofield's troops cut loose a vicious volley against 23,000 onrushing Rebs. It was a blood bath. The major wounds and loss of life for the unprotected, charging Southerners was devastating. The battle lasted through the night, and before dawn, Schofield withdrew from Franklin and headed north. Hood's men had paid a high price for his rage-filled decision. Five generals were killed in the battle (another died later), five others were wounded and one was captured. The total Confederate casualties from that battle numbered more than 7,000 men; the Union lost 2,326.[87]

The 9th Indiana suffered their first significant casualties in this round of skirmishes.

Arbuthnot, John	Dearborn County, Indiana	Private, Co. K	mortally wounded at Franklin, Tennessee
Brown, William	Marion County, Indiana	Private, Co. L	killed at Franklin, Tennessee
Buskel, William	Marion County, Indiana	Private, Co. L	killed at Franklin, Tennessee
Hobson, Volney	Cadiz, Henry County, Indiana	Captain, Co. E	killed beneath the Railroad trestle on Liberty Pike, buried at Batson Cemetery, Henry County, IN
Macy, Henry B.	Dalton, Indiana	Private, Co. C	mortally wounded at Franklin, Tennessee, died March 9, 1865 in Nashville, Tennessee

Watts, James S	Hendricks County, Indiana	Private, Co. I	killed at Franklin, Tennessee, buried at Franklin section, grave #445 Stones River National Cemetery, Murfreesboro, Tennessee.

Forty-four-year-old Private John Wine of Company C, who was from Losantville, Indiana, was wounded in the left thigh during the battle and had his leg amputated that same day by 10th Indiana Cavalry Assistant Surgeon Joseph R. Culbertson from Waverly, Indiana. The doctor left his practice, his wife Mary, and his four children to serve the Union in April of 1864. The brutality of the war and unpleasant tasks required of a battlefield surgeon, such as amputating limbs, may have been too much for this family doctor because he went AWOL on July 1, 1865. His commission was revoked on July 7, 1865.

Other casualties for the 9th during this series of skirmishes include

Second Lieutenant James S. Bristow, Company L (Southport, Indiana), killed at West Harpeth, Tennessee.

Private Adrian Parsons, Company I, severely wounded at West Harpeth, Tennessee.

Private Benjamin F. Ricks, Company E (Cadiz, Henry County, Indiana), killed at West Harpeth, Tennessee.[88]

The Rebel troops who fought in and around Franklin, Tennessee on December 17–26, 1864 were under the command of General John Bell Hood. The Union troops were led by General George Thomas's Federal Cavalry divisions under the command of Major General James H. Wilson.

General John B.Hood Troops

17th Alabama Infantry

31st Alabama Infantry

55th Alabama Infantry

9th Arkansas Infantry

15th Arkansas Infantry

1st Georgia Infantry

34th Georgia Infantry

39th Georgia Infantry

42nd Georgia Infantry

43rd Georgia Infantry

65th Georgia Infantry

Point Coupee Battery,Louisiana

4th Louisiana Infantry

13th Louisiana Infantry

19th Louisiana Infantry

20th Louisiana Infantry

30th Louisiana Infantry

13th Mississippi Infantry

45th Mississippi Infantry[89]

General George Thomas Troops

7th Illinois Cavalry

16th Illinois Cavalry

9th Indiana Cavalry

10th Indiana Cavalry

2nd Iowa Cavalry

19th Pennsylvania Cavalry

2nd Tennessee Cavalry

32nd Iowa Infantry

Chapter 12

Food in the Field

Just prior to his death at Sulphur Branch Trestle, Sergeant Curtis W. Hancock, who transferred to the 10th Indiana Cavalry, Company K, from the 68th Indiana Infantry, sent a short note from Pulaski to one of his 10 sisters, Elizabeth, who lived just southeast of Milan in Moores Hill, Dearborn County, Indiana. He opened the note with a one line poem: "When this you see, remember me though many miles apart we be." A portion of his letter also spoke about his June 12, 1864 breakfast and his soldiers pay.

"I feel pretty good this morning. I felt like I would like to set down to some warm biscuits and tea this morning although we had a very good breakfast. Had fried potato's, fried beef and plenty of coffee. We have more coffee than we use and plenty of hardtack."

I can't say just what we get a month. Some say 28 and some say 22 dollars a month. I don't know which it is." [90]

Fried potatoes, fried beef, and coffee were certainly an excellent meal for the troops, but depending on the situation and the location, food supplies for the Union troops in the field varied greatly. Individual rations usually consisted of four parts: three-fourths pound of salt pork, a cut from the belly and sides of a pig that is cured in salt, one pound of hard bread, called hardtack; coffee; and sugar. During extended battles and days spent in pursuit of enemy troops, there were times when the men considered it fortunate to find time to eat. Most of the men had limited cooking skills and found themselves on their own when it came to cooking the hunk of pickled pork.

Some of the soldiers fashioned a cooking pot by attaching a wire to an empty tin can, and others put together a frying pan from discarded canteen halves and a green tree limb to serve as a handle. Some units formed small groups of men and attempted to make the chore of preparing meals a social occasion.

The options for preparing salt pork were severely limited and no matter the cooking process it was still salt pork. Little could be done with it other than frying it, boiling it, or adding it to a stew if you were fortunate enough to have anything to add to the greasy lump of meat. If there was no time for cooking the soldiers would be forced to eat it "as is," placing the salt pork between two pieces of hardtack to create a makeshift sandwich.

The troops would also occasionally receive salted beef, which was even less desirable than salt pork. The beef was so bad the men named it "salt horse." It was barely fit for consumption, so heavily saturated in salt that the men would often soak it overnight in a running stream to wash off as much brine as they could. Even worse, the meat was often so poorly packaged that when the rations reached the men, their next meal was already secreting an incredibly sickening smell. "Salt Horse" was so foul that on occasion soldiers would vent their frustration by pelting the commissary tent with chunks of the rancid meat. In exasperation they would sometimes hold a mock burial and lay the putrid stuff to rest, complete with contrived military honors.

The army-issued hardtack presented its own problems. This rations item was a cracker-like biscuit made of flour and water, and if you were lucky, a bit of salt or sugar. They were sturdy, filling and lasted a long time if kept dry. However, they had an uninviting appearance that raised questions about its origin. Unfortunately it was what they were given and they had to deal with it. If time was a problem, hardtack would have been eaten as issued but alternative means were preferred if time allowed. A favorite option was to break it up and soak it in water left from boiling meat, then frying it in pork grease to make a tasty homemade crouton. It was an army "in the field" favorite that became known among the Union troops as "skillygalee," an English word for paste.

The necessity to be creative with hardtack sprang up many times due to the condition of the ration when it was received. If it had been improperly packaged, it could show up either rock hard or soaking wet and covered with mold. If it was not hard or wet it may have been full of weevils, and occasionally maggots, requiring more creativity on the part of the men. They found that the best solution was to use their freshly prepared hot coffee. The infested hardtack would be dropped into the boiling brew. After a short while, they could ladle off the dead bugs as they rose to the top. It was a perfect solution. They were rid of the weevils, and the uninviting hardtack was now soft and coffee-flavored. The really fortunate troops were treated to fresh meat only when the chief commissary of the army hired special drivers to herd beef cows behind the field armies and the cattle were slaughtered and issued to the troops. If time allowed, the soldiers prepared the meat for that day's march. The men usually cooked the fresh beef over campfires, a huge improvement over the stomach-turning salted meats.

The Government eventually addressed the problem of miserable army rations and attempted to upgrade the nutritional value of the rations by issuing what army regulations called "desiccated [dehydrated] compressed potatoes" and "desiccated compressed mixed vegetables." Soldiers were instructed to take the cubes of potatoes, turnips, carrots, and assorted greens and mix them with water. In theory, they re-hydrated and made a wholesome vegetable or vegetable medley. With few exceptions, the Yanks despised "desiccated" vegetables, which they labeled "desecrated vegetables" or "baled hay."

Although the army made an effort to improve rations throughout the war, the inconsistency of delivery and the quality of the rations forced the men to look for additional sources of food. Times of desperation fueled resourcefulness, and when the opportunity arose, the men would forage for supplemental or replacement food for their limited and repulsive army rations.

The 9th Indiana Cavalry's creativity in foraging had to rank near the top of Indiana units. Company D and John King's Company F were stationed around the Pulaski, Tennessee area, and on September 8, 1864, they were issued half rations for a 15 day period. Three days later, the hungry troops shot a random wandering hog, butchering it that night for the next day's meals. A few days after that, they killed two roaming cows. The next victim was another old sow. Other foraging included a six-mile round trip for some peaches and the killing of a couple more cows before receiving a second 15 day issue of rations. That load of supplies came 37 days after the last 15 day issue.

The men continued to forage when they could, but in late October they were eating bread and coffee for supper and hardtack and coffee for breakfast. By early November, the horses were suffering as well. As the hunger pangs grew, another foraging trip became necessary. Near Hortonsville, the men rounded up some cabbage, a goose, and some chickens and bagged a prize 200-pound hog. When they moved out the next morning, they grabbed a couple more geese to take with them.

By mid-December, the horses were down to one feed of oats a day. The men of the 9th were completely out of rations and had not received bread for three days. The foraged food was long gone and the starving troops were forced to survive by eating parched corn. It was often feast or famine for the men of the 9th Indiana Cavalry. [91]

As bad as it was for the Union Army, the Rebel rations bordered on criminal. The hardtack issued to the Southern troops was so hard, some of the soldiers broke their teeth while trying to eat it. The hard-as-brick rations generated some uncomplimentary nicknames, including "teeth-dullers," "sheet-iron crackers," "flour tile," and "ship's biscuit" were some of the favorites. Because the hardtack was often full of maggots and weevils, the men also dubbed them "worm castles." Coffee was a staple and just as highly regarded by the Union troops. However the Reb's were frequently forced to improvise by using chicory, the root of the endive lettuce plant, or roasted acorns. The substitutes were acidic and tasted terrible, but they drank what they had.

When food and other supplies were late, minimal, or non-existent for long periods of time, the men became desperate. With no idea if and when rations would be delivered, the starving Rebel troops would sometimes resort to eating their horses and mules. When the lack of food became life-threatening, some of the troops would catch and consume rats.

In a letter to his sister written in March of 1863 while camped in Vicksburg, Mississippi, 25-year-old Rebel Private Augustus Murrell Lillard of the 59th Tennessee Mounted Infantry, Company

B from Sweetwater, Tennessee, wrote,

> *"I have never been dissatisfied since I've been in service till I*
> *came to this place, which is enough to dissatisfy any person*
> *to have to do as much duty on so little to eat. Our beef is so*
> *poor that I do believe that one of our Tenn. farm hogs would*
> *refuse to eat it. We draw cornmeal and that's very coarse*
> *and not sived. You wrote you heard we was about to starve.*
> *I expect you heard nearly rite for I have actually suffered for*
> *something to eat."*

Private Lilliard wrote letters home regularly but in early June
of 1864, they stopped. His family received nothing for nearly three
weeks, until they received the following letter.

> *Camp Morton Indianapolis, Indiana June 27th1864*
> *Dear Sister,*
> *I have no doubt you all would like to learn something of*
> *my whereabouts. I am here a prisoner of war, was captured*
> *5th June at battle of Piedmont. My health has been very*
> *good. I need some money and would like for mother to send*
> *me $20 or $25 (U.S. money) and send it by express as it will*
> *not be safe otherwise.*
>
> *I want you to write very often as you are not allowed to*
> *write but one page and no news or nothing of the kind.*
>
> *I send you and Julia two rings I made in prison. Have*
> *you heard anything of brother Jack if you have give me his*
> *address. My love to all friends especially the Girls and would*
> *be very glad for any to write that will. Write me how the*
> *farm is doing and where the boys are and the health of the*
> *family and people generally.*

My love to all, accept a portion for yourself
Your brother
A.M. Lillard, Prisoner

His letters continued during his imprisonment asking about family, asking for clothing and money, and saying his health was fine.

Just prior to his enlistment Private August may very well have been ill. In 1861, he spent some time at the White Cliff Springs Tennessee Health Spa, where "healing" mineral water treatment was offered in the belief that it had curative powers to heal various ailments. [92]

Although his letters continued to tell his family he was in good health, he died at Camp Morton of a fever on November 22, 1864 and was buried with other deceased prisoners in Greenlawn Cemetery on November 30, 1864. After the war, the Greenlawn Cemetery land was sold to the railroad and all Confederate remains were moved to a mass grave in Section 32 of Crown Hill Cemetery. [93]

The morning of December 1, 1864, after only one hour of sleep, John King and the rest of the 9th Cavalry began the daily chore of caring for the horses while breakfast was being prepared. Before John was able to sit down and eat, nearby rifle fire was heard and a cavalryman rode into camp shouting, "The enemy is upon us!" The men immediately mounted their horses and waited for their orders. The rear guard of General John Bell Hood's command had discovered the camp and was on the attack.

Companies D and G of the 9th Indiana Cavalry, under the command of Major Virgil Lyon from Plainfield, Indiana, were instructed to move up the ridge and soon disappeared from sight. Company E was ordered to move out onto the road to watch for enemy troops coming that way. Some of the men were ordered to dismount and take a position behind a nearby house and instructed to fire once or twice if the enemy approached then fall back to their horses.

Within minutes the Reb's opened up a devastating volley of rifle fire from a nearby hill. Following orders, Company E fired their rounds and retreated to their horses, but the men in charge of their mounts had been ordered to the rear and had taken the horses with them. With no horses and no support nearly all of the abandoned men were captured. Twenty-six of them were sent to the prison in Cahaba, Alabama and then to Andersonville prison, where half of the men died within five months.

During that first barrage of bullets, a horse went down, one man was shot, and a second horse dropped to the ground.

The horses of Privates William Wheeler, Frank Sanford and Ed Wood were all killed. Wheeler said, "Mine was shot through the hip and the heart, and I lost all my traps." "Traps," were wide leather belts that held items such as the cap box, cartridge box, bayonet scabbard, a sack used to carry three days' rations, a tin cup, a plate, and a canteen.

As the Yanks were attacked, the men were ordered to dismount and take cover behind a nearby stone wall. The troops were relatively safe but the horses paid a price. The Rebels continued to pour in rifle fire and began a barrage of artillery fire from a small portable cannon known as a "jackass battery." The 9th did what they could, returning fire with their Maynard carbines. The Maynard rifle was a weak weapon that was useless at long Range. But because it was a breech loader, the 9th was able to return fire with such speed that the enemy overestimated the number of Union troops and hesitated to make a charge. The Rebs opted to sneak around both sides of the Union flanks in an attempt to surround the Yanks. At about the same time the Reb's made their move the 9th had fired their last shots and were now out of ammunition.

Adjutant Payne from General Hammond's staff was on hand and gave the order to retreat. The Union troops were nearly surrounded, had no ammunition, and had more men than horses. The Reb's were in control of the area. It was a critical situation.

Hurrying to the rear, the 9th Indiana men of companies D and G quickly mounted the available horses. Those without a mount rode behind a fellow cavalryman or held onto a stirrup or horse's tail to keep up with the retreating unit. They raced through woods and fields and over rail fences. From behind and either side came the hissing of bullets and again the Rebel yell. To the great surprise and relief of the retreating troops the rest of the 9th Regiment Cavalry troops, including Private John King, were waiting for both them and the enemy. The Union troops soon gained the upper hand; the enemy troops were routed and forced to retreat.

After this skirmish, the regrouped men of the 9th moved slowly toward Nashville until night came on. They made camp beside the main road and John and his fellow Cavalrymen bedded down for the night. Those who could sleep did.

For the rest of December, the men of the 9th moved and made camp around that same area of Tennessee. The winter of 1864-65 was the coldest that had been seen for many years and the men of the 9th began to see a stretch of temperature extremes in the Tennessee mid-winter weather. The week following their first taste of battle, it resembled an early spring; the weather stayed clear and warm. It didn't last. Temperatures dropped below freezing causing the men to suffer as they shivered in their tents at night. Rain began to fall, soaking the men, their equipment, and their clothing. The cold rain soon turned to sleet and then to snow as the temperature continued to drop. The overcoats of the 9th Indiana troops froze so thoroughly that they became stiff.

Rain and sleet continued through the following week, causing roads to become slippery and the men and horses susceptible to slipping, falling, and serious injury. Eventually there was a brief break in the cold snap but the warmer weather created yet another problem: The mud on the ground quickly grew to be nearly knee-deep. The horses were slowed to a snail's pace and the troops were unable to walk in the area without having their boots pulled off their feet.

On the evening of December 14, 1864, the men heard the sounds of nearby—heavy rifle fire and occasional cannon fire. That evening, as they anticipated their next encounter with the enemy, the men learned they were out of wood for their campfires, forcing another bitter, cold, miserable night in the field.

The next morning, with little sleep, the brigade moved out at 9:00 a.m. with the infantry and the artillery in front and the cavalry following them.

They soon encountered General Hood's Rebel forces and attacked them. The battle was brutal and lasted all day as both sides gave no ground during the nine-hour skirmish. At this point the Union cavalry realized there was now a shortage of horses so some of the riders were forced into battle on foot. Once new mounts arrived and the cavalry troops became organized, they were able to force the enemy to withdraw. Eventually, Hood's army retreated from that position after Union General John McArthur's 1st Division caused a collapse of the Rebel left flank.

After sustaining a severe loss of men to deaths, injuries, and capture, Hood and his remaining troops took off for the city of Franklin.

On December 16, 1864, John and the other troops of the 9th were up at 4:00 a.m. and on the march. Almost immediately, they encountered and attacked a small element of enemy troops in a close range skirmish. The Rebs began to fire "Buck," which consisted of one .69-ball and three buckshot. At close range, this "buck and ball" was like a shotgun and devastating to the enemy. The Confederates were only able to launch a small amount of artillery before the 9th made a charge.

Overwhelmed, the Rebs retreated about two miles before scaling a small mountain. When the 9th arrived at the site, it became obvious that the horses would not be able to make the climb. The men were ordered to dismount and charge up the steep incline on foot. When they reached the top the 9th chased the Reb's down the other side, across a cornfield, and over a second hill. It was now getting dark and the troops on both sides were totally exhausted. The chase was called off and the men set up camp for the night in an area known as Hollow Tree Gap. [94]

The next day, December 17, 1864, the fighting continued in and around Hollow Tree Gap, which was about four miles north of Franklin, Tennessee. Although the Rebs were vulnerable and on the run, they were certainly not defeated—as the Union troops soon learned.

As the 19th Pennsylvania and the 10th Indiana Cavalries continued the chase, they ran into a significant and determined group of ragged, worn-out Confederate Infantry, who were in position and waiting for them. It was a brutal battle. The Rebel troops managed to capture 63 prisoners and 22 Yanks were killed or wounded, most from the 10th Indiana. After the battle, one Union cavalryman said, "The illy clad shivering prisoners had led us to the conclusion that we had a walkover. Hollow Tree Gap undeceived us." [95]

At this point, the 9th Indiana Cavalry was ordered to take the advance. As they moved forward, they encountered a disheartening and emotional scene. A Union trooper lay on the ground, gasping his last breath. Beside him lay a sixteen-year-old curly haired, blue-eyed boy, Duane Lewis, the general's orderly. His innocence had made him a favorite of every soldier in the brigade. The young man had enlisted in Hancock County, Indiana, where he lived with John and Elizabeth Kester. The merciless rain fell on his youthful, upturned face. His eyes were open, but life was gone from this too-young soldier. [96]

As the Confederate troops were continuing their retreat, Private Phillip D. Stephenson, loader of piece number four for the 5th Washington Artillery in the Army of Tennessee, reflected on the demoralizing event. He later wrote,

"It must have been a strange, heart-sickening sight to the bewildered women and children lining the gates and porches and windows, as we passed by, to see us so soon retracing our steps, in such a plight. Gazing silently at us, a jostling herd of haggard men, equally silent ourselves, they stood, as column after column went by. What were their thoughts, their feelings? The rain still poured in torrents upon us, more dogged in its pitiless pursuit than the enemy. It still beat us down, as it had been doing day and night, day and night, ever since the day of our defeat, until the drops felt like heavy shot upon our heads. No sound save its merciless pour, and the slushy tramp of that miserable multitude hurriedly wading with bent forms and straining eyes

through the freezing mud, and the demonical howl of the ferocious wind." [97]

The Union troops were, of course, facing the same miserable weather conditions, but when you have ample supplies and are the aggressor, you notice the weather just a little bit less.

The situation for the Southern troops was indeed dire. If the Union troops managed to overtake them the options for the men in the Army of Tennessee were to be captured or to die in battle.

The 9th Indiana Cavalry continued their unrelenting pursuit of Hood and became involved in a brief skirmish at Lynville, Tennessee on December 23, 1864. [98] That same day, as the Confederate troops moved on, John and his fellow cavalrymen chased them through Spring Hill where, during an earlier skirmish on November 30, 1864, Private John Thompson of Company C, 124th Indiana Volunteers was captured by the Rebs.

Private John Thompson was another young Indiana enlistee. Originally from Kentucky, he was 15 years old in 1860 and living with his grandmother in Delaware Township in Hamilton County, Indiana prior to volunteering. John Thompson and John King would later cross paths; even with a considerable age difference they would become friends who later would share the emotions of euphoric happiness and agonizing heartbreak. [99]

During this pursuit of Hood, Wilson's Cavalry came upon the Confederate rear guard. The Rebel unit was easily driven back and sustained a considerable loss in soldiers, a mix of killed, wounded, and captured. Amazingly, there were no Union casualties.

The Rebel officers were now desperate to find a way to slow the Union pursuit long enough for the main body of their army to make its escape across the Tennessee River. Lieutenant General John

Bell Hood decided he would have Major General Nathan Bedford Forrest guard the rear of the Army of Tennessee to facilitate his retreat as the Union troops continued the chase. Forrest made his way to Devil's Gap, a narrow gorge in Anthony's Hill (also known as King's Hill) that was about seven miles from Pulaski, leaving part of his command to burn the bridge over Richland Creek. However, the 5th Iowa Cavalry charged Jackson's men and were able to douse the fire and save the bridge. Colonel T.J. Harrison of the 8th Indiana Cavalry quickly ordered two pieces of artillery into position with the troops stationed along the bank of the creek. His plan worked and the Reb's were again on the run.

When the Union troops caught up to them, the Reb's were in position and ready. Three concealed cannons were fired at the Yanks followed by a charge from two lines of infantry and a column of cavalry. Now it was the Union troops making a rapid retreat. The Yank's fell back for half a mile and Harrison's skirmishers regrouped. After receiving some support, his skirmishers held the enemy in check and again forced the Rebs to move out just as dark was coming on.

On the evening of December 24, 1864, John and his fellow troops were exhausted. The chase had been a mixture of steep hills and deep valleys that took a toll on the men and their horses. When the men were ordered to make camp for the night, Private King realized they were bedding down within sight of the block house where he was stationed prior to being issued a horse and re-joining his unit.

Christmas day of 1864 was a cloudy Sunday with drizzling rain.

The Reb's had moved into the town of Pulaski. Counting on making good on his escape, Forrest ordered his troops to the town square and told them to throw large stacks of clothing, bacon, and boxes of ammunition into a pile and set them on fire. As the flames scorched and burned the discarded items, women and children were seen watching from their windows and weeping at the scene. Forrest and his men moved south out of Pulaski.[100]

The Union troops continued to put pressure on the enemy. John and the other men were up at 4:00 a.m. and on the road. They marched through Pulaski and by afternoon were within just a few miles of the town borders before running into Forrest's skirmishers. Major General James H. Wilson quickly sent three regiments of dismounted Union cavalry into a wooded gorge leading up to Anthony's Hill. Forrest had posted two brigades of infantry and two brigades of cavalry with some field pieces, positioning them along a rail barricade. The Confederates began unleashing heavy fire, causing the Union troops to retreat with Forrest's men pursuing. The Confederates captured some cannons and after chasing the Union troops for another half-mile, they ran into a full division of Union cavalry. Forrest disengaged at this point, pulling his troops back up the hill to their original positions behind their barricades. After dark, the Confederates withdrew and made their way south to a small stream known as Sugar Creek, where Forrest hoped he could make a final stand that would allow Hood's army to complete the final 40 miles of its retreat to the Tennessee river.[101]

Due to the constant movement and the disarray of the entire Confederate system, Forrest's troops had long been without a supply line. Many of his men were now running and fighting in their bare feet which had become so cold and swollen that walking was extremely painful for the Rebel troops. To add to their misery, the weather turned freezing cold and the men were pelted with a cruel mix of hard sleet and light snow. In an effort to find some kind of relief the men wrapped pieces of blankets around their feet and tied them in place with leather thongs or rags.

After observing the extreme hardship and suffering of his men, Forrest finally ordered a few of the wagons to be emptied and let some of the men ride; the Yankees were still gaining ground.

The main road at that time took the armies through the community of Appleton in the southeastern corner of Lawrence County. The condition of the turnpike was as bad as any army ever tried to travel. Horses had to be pushed through knee-deep mud and slush, the exhausted bare-footed men marched on through ankle-deep, ice-cold water while the freezing sleet continued to beat upon their heads. [102]

On Christmas day of 1864, the 9th Indiana Cavalry continued to pressure the Reb's by forcing their enemy's rear guard back into the main body which was in a strong position on the south bank of Sugar Creek. The two armies spent the night on opposite sides of the creek, just east of Granny White Pike. [103]

The freezing Christmas-night bivouac at Sugar Creek was just another hardship for the 9th Indiana. In some ways, this special holiday was not much better for some of the civilian population of both the North and the South. The families left behind were all suffering their own adversity while fathers, husbands, and sons were off at war.

The holiday season was a distressing and gloomy time for John King's family back in Indianapolis. His wife Katherine, like many mothers in other states, had to make the best of a bad situation. Raising and caring for Wesley, Nettie, and baby George by herself, she was forced to rely on family and friends for whatever help they could provide.

In some areas of the South, parents faced a much more difficult situation as the war took place in and around their homes and cities. Facing near-hopeless conditions, some mothers told their children that "Santa was a Yankee" and that the Confederate pickets would not let Santa through the lines and because of this, there would be no Christmas.

A few southern families were blessed with a special Christmas thanks to 90 Union soldiers from Michigan who loaded up wagons with food and other supplies and passed them out to impoverished households throughout the Georgia countryside. The mules pulling the wagons were dressed up with tree branches tied to their ears to resemble reindeer. The kindness of a few Yankees gave those Southern children a special Christmas and a special memory. [104]

In the 1860s, Christmas was just beginning to be a more public activity as well as the traditional religious observance it had always been. Christmas cards were exchanged, people sang carols in public venues and cities were decorated with greenery in both the North and the South.

Some homes decorated trees indoors, and children were treated to a reading of "T'was the Night Before Christmas," a story that was originally published anonymously in 1823 and titled "A Visit From St. Nicholas."

As the war dragged on, there were fewer provisions of every kind available in both the North and South. With the men and boys away at war, home life for some of the families was a sad and stressful affair. Despite these hardships, on Christmas Eve of 1864, the *Indianapolis Daily Evening Gazette* newspaper carried articles on holiday activities in the city and ran ads for local storeowners promoting their merchandise.

One article reported
that the Christian Chapel
was having an event for
their young people and
their teachers at which they
decorated a Christmas tree
with food and gifts and
allowed the attendees to
strip the decorated tree of its

Downtown Indianapolis, 1864

bounty. The Masonic Hall and the German Presbyterian Church both
held festivals and one reporter was quoted as saying, "We understand
from those present that they had a good time generally." That rousing
endorsement by the reporter may indicate he was not impressed.

In the city at that time was well-known actor Joseph Proctor,
known as the American Tragedian, who was giving his final
appearance of the season at the Metropolitan in Indianapolis in a
play titled "*Robbers.*" The Metropolitan first opened at the corner
of Tennessee and Washington streets in 1859 and was the first
Indianapolis building dedicated only to theatrical activities.

The Morris Family grocery, located opposite the post office,
suggested in its advertisements that you come in early and get your
Christmas turkeys, flour, celery, raisins, nuts, and butter. Werden and
Company, a book and stationary store on east Washington Street
offered a good supply of Christmas wrapping paper. The Williams
and Van Camp Fruit House on Ohio Street, west of the canal,
advertised Catawba grapes in prime order and of the best quality,
retail or wholesale, along with apples and various canned fruits. [105]

Chapter 13

The Capture at Sugar Creek

Celebrating the Christmas holiday of 1864 was not on the mind of Gilbert Van Camp's brother-in-law John King on the morning of December 26. He had spent a restless and freezing night bivouacked next to Sugar Creek. Christmas had been just another day and another battle for the soaking wet and miserably cold trooper whose only dream that night may well have been of survival.

When John awoke early the morning of the 26th he found that a thick fog had settled in overnight, coming off the creek and settling in over the campsite. But there was a battle to be fought. Despite the conditions, the 9th Indiana officers were determined to keep the pressure on the Reb's. John and his fellow cavalrymen were called forward and lined up in preparation for a charge across the freezing water to attack the enemy troops who were camped about 100 yards to the south. The order was given and despite a restless, wet, and freezing night, John King urged his horse forward. He was just one frightened soul among the mass of other exhausted Union and Rebel troops as their horses broke through the ice, splashing across the freezing-cold water of Sugar Creek, and made their way up the bank to the opposite side.

The Confederates were waiting and ready for them. Forest had moved on and left Brigadier General Lawrence Ross in command. General Ross spent the night devising his battle plan. He later filed a report that described the scene on that foggy, damp, and bitter-cold day.

"Early on the morning of December 26th, the Yankees, still not satisfied, made their appearance and our Infantry made dispositions to receive them. Our two Infantry Brigades took position and immediately behind them had the two Cavalry units, the Texas Legion and the 9th Texas drawn up in columns of fours to charge, if an opportunity should occur. The fog was very dense and the enemy therefore approached very cautiously. When they were near enough to be seen, the Infantry fired a volley and charged. At the same time the Legion and the mounted 9th Texas were ordered forward and passing through our Infantry, crossed the creek in the face of terrible fire, overthrew all opposition on the farther side, and pursued the thoroughly routed foe for nearly a mile, killing a fair number of Yanks besides capturing twelve prisoners and as many horses." One of the captured prisoners was Private John H. King. [106]

Private Anderson Pinion, John's friend and fellow Company F Cavalryman, was with him in the heavy fog and the confusion of the battle and was captured at the same time. He told this story about how the two of them met their fate: "He [John] was hit in the battle we was in by a spent ball in the breast. I was beside him when he fell and said he was shot and he asked me to help him on his horse and I dismounted to help him and the enemy charged us and we was both captured." [107]

Now in the hands of the Third Texas Cavalry, the two of them were in a "good news, bad news" situation. The good news was they had survived the action at Sugar Creek. The bad news was they were to be sent to the Confederate prison camp in Sumter County, Georgia known as Andersonville Prison. One year and three days after his enlistment, John was still alive, but on his way to hell. Following the skirmish at Sugar Creek, Major General George H.

Thomas's troops continued their pursuit, but another strong stand by Hood's men stalled the Union Army.

After nearly a month of pursuit and a continuous retreat by the Confederates, General Forrest and his starving, exhausted, and outnumbered men escaped safely across the Tennessee River and into Alabama. [108]

Henry County, Indiana farmer Robert Crandall and his wife Elsie had three young sons serving in Company E of the 9th Indiana Cavalry in this campaign. The three of them—Andrew, James, and Rial, also known as Wyatt— left behind five brothers and four sisters when they made their commitment to

9th Indiana Cavalry Battle Route

the Northern cause, enlisting in September of 1863. Wyatt was captured by the enemy on the first of December and sent first to Cahaba prison, and then to Andersonville. James and Andrew survived the battle at Sugar Creek and both completed their service. James lived until August of 1896. Andrew later became an invalid before dying in July of 1901. [109]

The 9th Indiana battled Hood's troops from December 17 to December 26 of 1864 and suffered a loss of 12 good men from their ranks. That number included nine dead and two severely wounded from six different Indiana counties that ranged from Kosciusko County in the middle of the northern portion of Indiana to Dearborn County in the southeast part of the state.

9th Indiana Cavalry Killed and Wounded

December 17–26, 1864

John Arbuthnot, Dearborn County, Indiana. Private, Co. K. Mortally wounded at Franklin, Tennessee

James S. Bristow, Southport, Indiana. Second Lieutenant, Co. L. Killed at West Harpeth, Tennessee

William Brown, Marion County, Indiana, Private, Co. L. Killed at Franklin, Tennessee

William Buskel, Marion County, Indiana. Private, Co. L. Killed at Franklin, Tennessee

Volney Hobson, Cadiz, Henry County Indiana. Captain, Co. E. Killed beneath the railroad trestle on Liberty Pike, north of Franklin, Tennessee on the morning of December 17, buried at Batson Cemetery, Henry County, Indiana

Duane A. Lewis, Fortville, Indiana. Private, Co. B. Killed at Hollow Tree Gap

Henry B. Macey, Dalton, Indiana. Private, Co. C. Mortally wounded at Franklin, Tennessee; died March 9, 1865, Nashville, Tennessee

Adrian Parsons, Washington, Hendricks County Indiana. Private, Co. I. Severely wounded at West Harpeth, Tennessee on December 17, 1864 and admitted to Hospital #8, Nashville, Tennessee

Benjamin F. Ricks, Cadiz, Henry County, Indiana. Private, Co. E. Killed at West Harpeth, Tennessee

James S. Watts, Hendricks County, Indiana. Private, Co. I. Killed at Franklin, Tennessee, buried at Stones River National Cemetery, Murfreesboro, Tennessee—Franklin Section, grave #445

Jacob Wine, Monroe, Kosciusko, Indiana. Co. C. Wounded in left thigh at West Harpeth Tennessee on December 17, 1864. Leg was amputated the same day (anterior post. flap) by Assistant Surgeon

J.R. Culbertson, 10th Indiana Cavalry, who was discharged May 15, 1865[110]

Chapter 14

Andersonville

There are some very graphic descriptions of Andersonville prison, none of which adequately describe the suffering, degradation, and filth of this Rebel prison camp. One account lists it as a hastily built Southern stockade that was glutted with humanity and had become a reeking, lice-infested, scurvy-ridden, maggot-breeding pest hole of suffering and death.

There were many contributing factors to the conditions at Andersonville. Conditions that created a situation that no living creature should be forced to endure. Because an exchange of prisoners would have prolonged the war, during negotiations the US Government presented the South with a list of difficult and nearly impossible demands with which they could not comply. As a result, the South became burdened with thousands of Union prisoners at a time when its own troops were without food, weapons, or clothing. [111]

As the war progressed, the Southern prison camps in the East became more vulnerable to Yankee troops. As a preventative measure, the Rebs decided to build a prison camp in the Deep South, away from the possibility of attack. Captain Richard B. Winder was assigned as quartermaster for the camp and given the unenviable task of constructing the prison at Andersonville.

The original stockade enclosed about sixteen and a half acres and was fenced by pine trees that had been cut down, trimmed, and topped to a length of about 20 feet. The local Negroes hewed the logs to a thickness of eight to 12 inches and placed them five feet into the ground, making a wall approximately 15 feet high. [112]

Beyond these pine trees, Captain Winder's ability to obtain building materials was almost nonexistent. The local mill operators would not sell him wood because of more lucrative sales to the Southern government for use on desperately needed railroads.

He submitted a request for tents for the prisoners, but was informed by the Confederate quartermaster that the tents could not be supplied because they did not have any tents. He was instructed to buy beef in Florida and southern Georgia, but Winder didn't have enough men to drive the stock and there was no other way to get them. His orders also said he should call upon the nearest commissary for supplies, but this was in Columbus, which was 50 miles away.

In the midst of this dilemma, and with the stockade only about half completed, the first batch of 500 prisoners arrived on Thursday, February 25, 1864. [113] Unable to provide even the basic necessities of food, shelter, and clothing, the prison began an immediate downhill slide into an unbelievable condition.

About a month after the prison opened, Captain Henry J. Wirz, who had been appointed commandant of the prison, arrived to take charge of the complex and its prisoners. Wirz had a basically useless right arm from a war wound and was no longer fit for frontline duty so he was assigned to Andersonville, where he began his tenure as an abusive and inhumane dictator. He had a volatile, unpredictable temper and was described as a brutal coward who had no compunction for humanity and an unfeeling conscience. The addition of Captain Wirz to the prison only added to the problems and misery of the environment. [114]

There was no orderly plan or discipline of any kind at the prison. With only open ground and no housing, the men constructed "shanties" from the few odds and ends they could find. Sticks, limbs, rags, clothing, bushes, and shrubs were used to fend off the scorching Georgia sun and the violent summer storms. The prisoners followed their own personal whims as to where they located their huts, and consequently, there were no direct aisles or streets. Making your way around the camp was like negotiating a maze.

A branch of Sweetwater Creek flowed through the prison and was originally to be the water source for the prisoners, but the cookhouse was near a tributary to the creek and the garbage, refuse, and any other trash, was thrown into the water source for the prisoners.

A latrine, or "sinks," as they were called, was built next to a portion of the west wall and right next to the creek. In addition to the cookhouse, the prisoners, with no other option, contaminated the stream with their own bodily wastes and personal garbage and trash. What had once been a small flowing stream became a sluggish, semi-liquid mass of germ-infested filth.

Eventually the ill and dying men were too weak to make it to the "sinks" and began urinating and defecating right at the entrance to their shanties, next to where they cooked their food. The stench of the prison became overwhelming and permeated the countryside for miles around. Near the camp cooking area was a mound of rotting garbage and trash of all kinds that was 30 feet in diameter, several feet high, and swarming with flies. The flies crawled over the faces and bodies of the men and many prisoners were so covered with mosquito bites that they appeared to be suffering from measles. [115]

Typhoid and small pox were rampant and food supplies were nearly nonexistent. The men were starving. When food was available it was worse than poor in quality, never healthy, and often raw. If they wanted their food cooked, the prisoners had no choice but to make their own fires from whatever they could get their hands on. They started with the pine stumps left from the building of the prison as kindling for their fires and when those were gone they began digging up roots from the ground. On occasion in the early years of the camp small groups of prisoners were allowed to go outside the walls to scrounge for kindling, but after several escape attempts the "privilege" was revoked. After that, anything and everything became fair game. [116]

By the time John King arrived in late December of 1864, the prison had become a logistical and environmental nightmare. Salted meat and coarse unbolted cornbread were the mainstay of the prisoners' diets and the resulting cause of dysentery and diarrhea among the troops,[117] and it continued to get worse.

Joseph Stevens was born in Yorkshire, England in 1842 and had enlisted in Company E, 4th Michigan Infantry at Adrian, Michigan on June 20, 1861 and was another unfortunate Yank who ended up in Andersonville prison. When telling his story years later, he related an incident that could only be believed when told by one who had experienced it.

> *"The food they gave us was corn cobs all ground up and made into mush and there wasn't near enough of that to keep the boys alive any length of time.*
> *Those that lived had to speculate by trading their brass buttons, boots, etc. with the guards. There were from one hundred to one hundred and fifty boys dying every day.*

A large wagon drawn by four mules was used in drawing out the dead. They were laid in a pile, as we pile cord wood, and taken to the burying ground generally putting fifty in a grave and returning would bring mush in the same wagon where worms that came from the dead could be seen crawling all over it, but we were starving, therefore we fought for it like hungry hogs." [118]

Prisoners receive daily rations.

Prisoners burying fellow prisoners

Private Eppenetus McIntosh was born in Terre Haute, Indiana in 1845 and later moved to Illinois, where he enlisted in the 14th Illinois Infantry. He served in Companies C and E before they were combined with Company A due to a significant loss of men in the other two units. Private McIntosh had been wounded three times. He was shot twice in the shoulder and once in the right foot.

On April 4, 1864, he was captured in a battle at a rail station in Acworth, Georgia. After a five-day forced march in a cold, drizzling rain, he arrived at Andersonville on October 9, 1864. He would survive with a story to tell and a picture that made him famous. It was a photo that served as a testament to the Andersonville legacy.[119]

During the sizzling hot summer of 1864, a Catholic Priest, Father William Hamilton, visited the prison and reported upon leaving that he had seen prisoners burrowed into the ground like moles to protect themselves from the sun. The underground holes, he said, were alive with vermin and stank like "charnel houses" (burial vaults). In order to minister to them, he would have to "creep on his hands and knees into the holes that the men had burrowed into the ground and stretch himself out alongside of them to hear their confessions."

Many of the prisoners, he reported, were stark naked, having not so much as a rag to lie on or a garment to cover them. He immediately contacted his bishop and asked that a priest be assigned to the camp. The bishop agreed and chose Father Peter Whelan who was the chaplain for all Confederate forces in Georgia. He could not have made a better choice—Father Whelan gave it his all.

When Whelan arrived he was stunned by what he saw. Appalled at the condition of the prison area and the condition of the men, he decided he would begin living the life of the prisoners at Andersonville. He ate the same parched corn, cow peas, and coarse cornbread, drank their coffee, and slept in a miserable, filthy eight-by-twelve foot cattle shed. His day began inside the stockade at 5:00 a.m. and went until dusk. He comforted the sick, heard prisoners' confessions, gained converts, and administered last rites. Death came so fast and so often that Father Whelan was forced to shorten the sacramentalia, the baptisms, and the Extreme Unction.

Dysentery was the most fatal disease in the prison. The sick and dying men lay on the ground in their own excrement and vomit, the smell was so horrible that the good father was often forced to rush from their presence to escape the rancid air that surrounded the dying men. The polluted, unsanitary environment, coupled with the flies, mosquitoes, and body lice, created an environment so appalling that it took a brave, committed man to endure this wretched environment and provide a small amount of comfort and hope to the dying masses. [120]

Two Indianapolis boys described the extent of the lice infestation in their personal diaries. Private Lessel Long of Company F, 13th Indiana Infantry wrote, "There were about a dozen of us who went together and fixed up a place in one of the sheds which we called our own. There we remained several days and nights. The weather was very cold and having no clothing we suffered terribly. We would all lay down together and crowd up to each other as close as we could to get all the warmth possible, one from the other. In this way we spent our time, only getting out long enough to answer at roll call and draw our rations. After eating our scanty supply we would lay down and remain as quiet as we could. We had been here but a short time until we were bothered terribly with the greybacks [the Union Army term for lice]. As soon as we would begin to get a little warm they would commence their daily and nightly drill. They would have division, brigade, and regiment and company drills, ending up with a general review. When those large fellows began to prance around in front of the lines it would make some one halloo out, 'I must turn over, I can't stand this any longer.' So we would all turn to the right or the left as the case might be. This would stop the chaps for a short time."

Private William B. Clifton of Company K, 8th Indiana Cavalry wrote, "Well, we had to have some kind of amusement and didn't have anything to play with, so some of the boys got to racing lice. That got to be quite an amusement.

We would get a tin plate from someone and make a small ring in the center of the plate then make a ring around the cut edge of it, then heat it in the sun, drop the two lice in the center of the plate, and bet on the one getting out of the ring first. Someone would say drop and as soon as they struck the plate they would start and it was fun to see them run. There was two kinds of lice, some were dark, some slimmer and more round and lighter in color. One fellow had one that was the best. That fellow would have bet any money on it if he had it. I see poor fellows crawl up to look at the lice race that would be dead in thirty minutes, and I have seen them sitting up on the ground, their head between their hands, and fall over dead, lay there till the dead wagon came and hauled them out. September 23, 1864." [121]

After several distressing and heartrending months of service, Father Whelan was forced to leave Andersonville in October of 1864 after falling ill with a "lung ailment," possibly tuberculosis passed on by one of the inmates. As he left, he shared all of his remaining money with the starving, dying prisoners. He returned home, and even though he was broke, went to Macon and borrowed 16,000 Confederate dollars to buy bread for those he had left behind, saying, "My motive was not money; it was to allay misery and gain souls for God." [122]

As new prisoners continued to arrive at Andersonville, they were greeted by shouts of, "Fresh fish, fresh fish," and everyone who was able rushed to meet the latest crop of prisoners. In the beginning, the prisoners were anxious to ask where their new comrades were from, what unit they were with, and about the latest war developments and the latest news, bombarding them with questions from every direction. But the longer the men were exposed to these appalling prison conditions, the more their behavior deteriorated when greeting the newcomers.

As the horrors in the prison grew worse news from outside was no longer relevant. What was now important was survival, and the "fresh fish" became victims. It eventually came to a point where civility ended and mob mentality prevailed. They began rushing the new men, shoving and pushing each other to get close, and on many occasions they knocked down the new arrivals, trampling them and sometimes injuring them. As soon as the new prisoners entered the gate they were attacked by able prisoners who took everything they had, including their shoes and clothing, leaving their fellow Yankees bloodied and dazed on the ground. [123]

Newcomers were not the only ones in danger within the confines of Andersonville. A group of men had formed a gang of raiders who were absolutely ruthless and preyed upon the prison population. They would prowl the prison day and night and attack and rob their fellow inmates of their meager possessions, down to their last button or rag, clubbing them to death or slitting their throats in the process. They were a physical plague in an already diseased atmosphere.

The prison population endured this criminal and vicious activity until they'd had enough. A company was formed among the men with the goal of capturing the leaders of the notorious gang. The men, in desperation, solicited the help of Captain Wirz, who, after seeing one severely beaten man agreed to support their effort. The battle began.

After many head knocking, eye gouging, and clubbing skirmishes, the gang was broken up and six of the leaders were captured and turned over to Rebel officers for safekeeping. The other gang members were held by the prisoners in various areas of the camp.

The leaders of the emancipators then contacted Union General William Tecumseh Sherman to ask what they could do with the captured gang leaders. His reply was to "court martial them and do what you think best."

A court-martial board and a jury was selected from the Union prisoners and it was decided that the six men would be courts-martialed and sentenced to be hanged. The remaining gang members received a variety of sentences, including running the gauntlet, flogging, hanging by the thumbs, and having their heads shaved.

A scaffold was erected inside the stockade as the men prepared to carry out the death sentence. The six men were lined up in a row and a rope was placed around each of their necks. A minister from among the prisoners offered a prayer for them. When he finished, the trap fell. One of the ropes broke, and the freed man immediately took off running through the crowd. He was soon brought back and upon seeing the rest of his comrades hanging, pleaded for mercy. The cry from the troops was, "String him up!" He was put on the scaffold a second time and hung. The bodies were there until sundown so that the remaining gang members and everyone else could see what awaited anyone with similar ambitions. That evening, the men were cut down, stripped of their clothing, and buried in a single grave.[124]

By the end of February 1865 the unhealthy atmosphere, the quality of the water, the lack of food, and the everyday struggle to survive had taken its toll on John King. He was now in such a weakened condition that he was admitted to the camp hospital suffering from dibilitis, a condition of the body in which the vital functions are feebly discharged, more commonly known as dysentery. [125]

Sergeant James H. Kimberlin of the 124th Indiana Infantry, who had been a friend prior to the war and was also in charge of John's Indiana group at Andersonville, stated, "King contracted diarrhea, after which he was also attacked with scurvy, from which he suffered severely. In fact, for a time his life was almost entirely disposed of. I took special care of John and often went in person with him to the physicians in charge." [126] There were several options for treatment of John's condition but few were available in the undersupplied and undermanned prison hospital. Recommendations under normal circumstances included rest, change of air, generous feeding, and the proper medication. The rest was not a problem at the prison but the change of air, generous food, and nearly all of the medications were definitely out of the question. A variety of medicines were normally recommended for debilitis at that time. Lead acetate, opium, aromatic sulfuric acid, silver nitrate, belladonna, calomel, and ipecac were common, but without proper dosage and monitoring, some of them could be fatal.

In a typical Southern prison environment the most likely sources of treatment available, in some degree, were quinine, or one the men preferred, alcohol, which was typically whiskey or brandy. [127]

Whether John was fortunate enough to get a dose of quinine or a shot of liquor is not known, but by March 5, through some miracle, the doctors determined that John had improved and returned him to the prison area. The Camp hospital was far from being a clean environment. Food and beds were under-stocked and despite having been housed among the sickest of the sick, John would most likely preferred to have stayed there rather than return to the campsite with his 9th Indiana comrades.

Not all prisoners made it to the hospital because of their

weakened condition, even though sick call sometimes lasted up to six hours. When prisoners did make it to the hospital, it is questionable how beneficial it was for them. The doctor-to-patient ratio was over 200 to one. On several occasions during the second quarter of 1864, the hospital was without medicine of any kind and there was a shortage of beds. If you were lucky enough to have a bed, the odds were that you shared it with another prisoner. Some of the hospital tents had no beds and ill prisoners were forced to lie on the ground with no shelter at all.

The hospital "nurses" were paroled prisoners who were untrained and extremely negligent in caring for their sick comrades with varying stages of smallpox, typhoid, dysentery, diarrhea, malarial fever, and scurvy.

The absence of vitamin C and any kind of nutritional diet led to the scurvy which in turn became a fatal form of diarrhea or dysentery, the largest single cause of death in the camp.[128]

The sick and abused men appeared to be walking skeletons, causing Sergeant David Kennedy of the 9th Ohio Cavalry to observe, "It takes seven men to make a shadow."

Private Clay Terhune of the 9th Indiana Cavalry, Company A was an enlistee from Franklin, Indiana who had been captured at Sulphur Trestle, Tennessee and sent to Andersonville. In a strange twist of fate Terhune was captured at Sulphur Trestle by his Confederate cousin, James Euslich, the son of Clay's aunt, Anne Terhune. [129] He suffered badly from an inflammation to his lungs, which in most cases was caused by an infection from the surrounding filthy environment. Like so many of his fellow malnourished and untreated comrades, he succumbed to his illness and died February 7, 1865.

John King, still struggling, continued to suffer from his combination of dibilitis and scurvy. Constantly tired, he experienced muscle weakness, joint and muscle aches, a rash on his legs, and bleeding gums. These same miseries would plague him the rest of his life.

Thomas W. Horan, who lived in a log cabin on North Green River Road in Vanderburgh County prior to the war left his widowed mother to enlist in Company H, 65th Indiana Volunteers of the Union Army in August of 1862. He fought in several battles in Kentucky and Tennessee before being captured by the Texas Rangers near Tazwell, Tennessee. That was the beginning of an unimaginable experience.

Horan was shuttled from one southern prison to another. He realized what was in store for him early on, stating, "We were drove into a pen like hogs until we were marched into Russellville. That evening we took cars to Bristol, Virginia and arrived there that night. I will give a slight idea of our rations on this trip.

"When we arrived at Bulls Gap, they turned us out to help ourselves to beef, which was in great quantity but not quality, but we skinned and eat quite hearty of the beef heads that our forces left after butchering them some three weeks before. It had not a nice smell, I assure you, but it wasn't the smell we was after."

Horan's next stop was Bell Island, another wretched place in which men were dying daily from cold and hunger. The rations per day were two spoons full of beans and a small piece of cornbread. They had no blankets or shelter, and each group of twenty prisoners received only two sticks of cordwood for their fires each day and every night some of his fellow prisoners froze to death.

Horan became hopeful when he was pulled from that prison,

hoping he might be exchanged. Instead, he was loaded on a train and shipped to Andersonville.

Shortly after he arrived, he wrote home, saying, "If there is a hell on earth it's this one. Here I was turned in the stockade without a blanket or a shoe to my foot and the skies above me for shelter. During this time I saw sights and went through hardships too numerous to mention. During my stay in this place from 18 March to 13 September the number of deaths was 13 thousand and 800.

I have saw men lying not able to help themselves with maggots working in their wounds with them alive."

As the wretched days dragged on, Horan and a companion devised a plan to escape by tunneling under the log fence. To their surprise, they got away. The two men tramped through swamps with no shoes and lived on whatever they could find that was edible. They were eventually recaptured and returned to the Andersonville prison on a very sad Christmas Eve of 1864.[130]

As John King continued his fight to survive, deaths within the prison multiplied and the Confederate hierarchy became concerned. It was decided that an effort would be made to understand and hopefully resolve the problem. Their solution was to send Dr. Joseph Jones, professor at Princeton University in 1853, then a professor at the University of Pennsylvania Medical School, and later a professor at the Medical College of Georgia, to Andersonville. His assignment was to determine the true causes of the extreme mortality rate at the prison. Doctor Jones soon found that there was not just a single reason for the deaths but an alarming combination of gangrene, dysentery, and hookworm.

The larvae of the hookworm develop and survive in the environment of damp dirt and particularly in sandy and loamy soil that was prevalent in the filthy prison environment. The lack of any kind of sanitation, poor hygiene by the men, the home-built outhouses, and the polluted "sinks" added to the nurturing of the worms. When ingested or absorbed through the skin, the hookworm attaches itself to the lower intestine before being excreted by the men back into the soil.

This created a vicious cycle: The worms were absorbed by penetrating the skin of the men through bare feet, hands, while they were sleeping on the ground, inadvertently eating dirt, or drinking contaminated water. Eventually, nearly every inmate was infected. Hookworm is not necessarily fatal, but under those circumstances it became a serial killer. [131]

A second just as deadly health hazard was the issue of gangrene. In a report written by Doctor Jones, he stated, "In the foul atmosphere of the stockade and hospital the smallest injury such as a splinter, a small blister or even an abrasion from scratching a mosquito bite were often followed by the most extensive and alarming gangrenous ulceration. In this foul atmosphere even amputation would not arrest the gangrene. Nearly every amputation was followed by death." Gangrene also attacked the intestinal canals of the prisoners, which were raw from their corn-cob diet, causing severe ulceration of the bowels. Most cases ended in death without showing any outward signs of the disease.

After observing the prisoners' hopeless and pathetic situation, Dr. Jones's secretary wrote to his wife, "In my travels in China and various sections of the globe, I have witnessed many an awful sight and beheld the dead and dying in various stages. I even now recall to mind most vividly some fearful scenes of death within the prison of Shanghai and also cases of cholera in the north of China, but all is nothing to what I am now beholding." [132]

One of those sights was the daily hauling of bodies to the "dead house." The men would be piled on a cart, with multiple arms and legs and heads hanging over the wagon. The cadavers, with eyes glassy and mouths hanging open, were pushed along by other wretched souls who foresaw the dead and decomposing as their own fate. The bodies were taken out through the gates to the cemetery, where they would share a mass grave dug by their fellow Yankee prisoners. The bodies were covered with vermin, filthy from head to toe and covered with their own excrement and black soot from the smoke of the camp fires. [133]

Captured on July 22, 1864 at Decatur, Georgia, Private William Comfort of the 35th New Jersey Volunteers was another poor soul who had been sent to Andersonville. He faced the starving days, rainy and freezing nights, and the filth and disease that ran unchecked inside the prison.

After surveying the daily death toll and the brutal suffering of his comrades, Private Comfort was convinced he would meet the same grisly fate as the others, dying an agonizing death in a vile and heartless place and then being carted to the burial ground among a pile of other emaciated carcasses. He had lost all hope for life and felt betrayed by the government he'd pledged to serve. In this mood of despair, he scratched out a poem and poured out his heart:

"Have You Left Us Here To Die"
When our country called for men, we came from forge and store and mill.
From workshops, farm and factory, the broken ranks to fill;
We left our quiet homes and the ones we loved so well,
to vanquish all our union foes, or fall where others fell.

Now in prison drear we languish and it is our constant cry;
Oh ye who yet can save us, will you leave us here to die?
The voice of slander tells you that our hearts were weak with fear,
that all or nearly all of us were captured in the rear.
The scars upon our bodies from musket ball and shell,
the missing legs and shattered arm a truer tale will tell.
We have tried to do our duty in sight of god on high,
Oh ye who yet can save us, will you leave us here to die?
There are hearts with hopes still beating in our pleasant northern homes,
waiting, watching for the footsteps that may never, never come.
In a southern prison pining, meager, tattered, pale and gaunt, growing weaker,
weaker daily from pinching cold and want.
There, brothers, sons and husbands poor and hopeless captives lie,
Oh ye who yet can help us, will you leave us here to die?
Just outside our prison gate there is a graveyard near at hand,
where lie twelve thousand union men beneath the Georgia sand.
Scores and scores are laid beside them as day succeeds each day,
And thus it shall ever be until the last shall pass away.
And the last can say when dying with uplifted glazing eye,
Both faith and love are dead at home they have left us here to die.

In spite of his dire prediction, William Comfort was more

fortunate than most. On September 19, 1864, he was selected as an exchange prisoner and received his release in Atlanta, Georgia. By 1870, he was living in Trenton, New Jersey with his wife Rebecca and their two children, working as a laborer. By 1880, his wife had applied for a widow's pension. Comfort had died at home with his family, a far better fate than the one that awaited him had he stayed at Andersonville. [134]

At about that same time, 680 miles northwest of Andersonville, a local newspaper in St. Louis, the *Missouri Republican* published a report that the shipping business on the river was uncommonly slow. Some of the ship owners chose to dock their ships until business improved but those still in service faced stiff competition for the available business. Captain Cass Mason managed to get a share of the consignments for the *Sultana* but it wasn't enough to keep him solvent. In desperation he was forced to sell a portion of his three-eighths interest in the *Sultana*. When business failed to increase, he was forced to sell more of his personal ownership. By the time he was done, he was no longer a majority owner, but a minority owner with one-sixteenth of a share. His first clerk now owned a larger share of the *Sultana* than he did.

In the second week of April in 1865 while the weakening John King and his ailing and dying fellow prisoners were losing hope, the *Sultana* was docked at the wharf in Saint Louis, preparing for another run to New Orleans. Captain Mason was anxious to leave but was being held back by the local inspectors who were giving ships a mandated periodic safety check. The *Olive Branch*, owned by one of Mason's competitors, had already left the dock, giving them a day's advantage in the competitive battle for business.

He was hoping his two Irish bartenders, James O'Hara and

Thomas McGinty, would be able to soothe the passengers anxiety tomorrow after the one-day delay. Two men from the Board of Inspectors arrived on time the next morning and began their thorough inspection. The *Sultana* was now two years old and the inspectors wanted to examine the boilers which were always a concern in the muddy, trash-laden Mississippi.

When Captain Lodwick built the *Sultana*, he'd installed tubular boilers that were a newer design than many of the older boats.

The *Sultana* regularly ran the boiler pressure at 145 pounds; during the test it was pushed to 210 pounds and was stable. Convinced the ship was safe Inspectors gave Captain Mason his certification papers and told him he had permission to leave. With his cargo already on board, he loaded his passengers, pulled away from the dock, and headed down river. [135]

The once-proud South had now crumbled. Men of the Confederate Army were deserting, slaves had fled to the north, southern cities and towns had been burned along with the crops and barns, and the looming food shortage cut yet another notch into its list of problems.

Confederate President Jefferson Davis, confronted with an obvious and unpleasant situation, attempted a peace settlement with President Lincoln. Lincoln refused, saying the South must agree to a complete surrender. In April of 1865, the last line of the Confederate defense collapsed under General Ulysses Grant's army and Union troops marched into Richmond, the last bastion of the Southern government and troops.

The Rebs set fire to parts of the city as they fled, but the Confederate capitol was now in the hands of the victors. Within a few days, President Lincoln came to the city to honor the troops and acknowledge the city's defeat. On April 9, 1865, General Lee surrendered to General Grant at the Appomattox Courthouse in Virginia. The war was finally and officially over.

Confederate Private Gideon Luke Roach of the 63rd Regiment, 5th Cavalry, Company D, North Carolina Infantry from Caswell County, North Carolina, wrote a poem expressing his emotions for the Southern cause at the war's end, closing with this final verse:

The gates of time wide open stand,

And through them streams a deathless band--

Southern women, Southern men,

Who come to thrill our souls again;

And through the mist of tears we pray,

"God keep them all who loved the gray."

Gideon was quite a character; he later claimed to have been a captain in the Civil War but in truth he only made private. He went through three or four marriages in his lifetime, moving from North Carolina to Illinois to Indiana and then to California where he lived in a home for old soldiers. He and some of the healthy men were written up in a California newspaper and he claimed to be over 100 years old. After checking several censuses, it seems that he added a couple years onto his age in each new census.[136]

Chapter 15

The Death of Andersonville

Following the surrender of the Confederacy, the closing of Andersonville prison took place from mid-April to the first of May of 1865. Confederate Colonel and Post Commander George C. Gibbs of the 42nd North Carolina Volunteer Infantry, whose unit had done previous prison guard duty, was in charge of the release process. Andersonville records show that Gibbs released what was considered the last prisoners on May 4, 1865. However, they also show there were 22 prisoners still in the camp on May 5. Most likely, these were men who were near death or too ill to be moved. Later, when Federal troops arrived, a few former prisoners were still there, camped outside the prison walls.[137]

Dr. Amos Thornburgh, the assistant surgeon at Andersonville, completed his duties by sending a report of his observations and experiences with the medical situation at the prison to Dr. Joseph Jones. His feelings of helplessness and guilt were reflected in his closing paragraph in which he wrote, "Feeling we have done our whole duty, both in the eyes of God and man, we leave the matter to rest with those whose duty it was to furnish supplies and build up a hospital that might have reflected credit on the Government and saved the lives of thousands of our race."[138]

On April 22, 1865, a malnourished ill trooper from the 9th Indiana Cavalry passed away at the prison. Private George O. Huston Company D from Union, Indiana was captured during the same skirmish as John King at Sugar Creek, Tennessee but was too sick and weak to leave with the rest of his unit. He died just seven days after his friends and fellow troopers were released.[139]

Although the prisoners were officially liberated, the fatalities continued to soar. The remaining near death Union prisoners were left to wait for help and rescue by their government. By the time federal troops closed the prison at the end of April in 1865, 32,000 men had been imprisoned there and had suffered greatly. Of those 32,000 men, 13,000 had died, establishing a death toll of over forty percent.[140]

When the word came that the camp had been closed, John and his fellow prisoners were discharged with no special announcement or grand gesture of any kind. They were simply told they were released. The sick and dying men lined up and were marched to the nearby railroad to wait for a train to take them to Montgomery, Alabama.

Thomas Horan of the 65th Indiana Volunteers, the survivor of multiple prisons, said upon his release, "When the gate was opened I felt I could march fifty miles as poor and as weak as I was. When I was captured my weight was 175 pounds and when I was released I weighed 106 pounds. Thank God I am spared to return to the land of plenty." [141]

The heart breaking scene of the Andersonville release was described by Lieutenant Joseph T. Elliot of the 124th Indiana Infantry who had just spent the last two months in the Andersonville "officers' pen." "It was one of the most pitiful sights I ever beheld. Coming like cattle across an open field were scores of men who were nothing but skin and bones; some hobbling along as best they could and others being helped by stronger comrades. Every gaunt face with its staring eyes told the story of the suffering and starvation they had gone through, and protruding bones showed through their scanty tattered garments. One might have thought that the grave and the sea had given up their dead." [142]

John King was one of those skeletal souls and though he was now free from the confines of the prison the effects of the scurvy, the starvation, the diarrhea, as well as the diet of salted meat, ground corn cobs, and whatever else he managed to scrounge, had destroyed his health. The damage to his body would remain with him for life. Even in this misery his spirits must have been high. He had survived and was on his way home, not knowing more tragedy lay ahead.

When the transport train finally arrived, the strongest of the men fought amongst themselves trying to get on board. It was every man for himself. Many of the men had an overwhelming fear that he might somehow be left behind and returned to the nightmare of the Rebel prison camp. Some caring souls held back and patiently helped the weak and infirm on board, making them as comfortable as the conditions would allow.

During the slow ride to Montgomery, Alabama, John was a witness to more death as nearly every depot they passed became a place to drop off those who had died between stops. The locals from each stopover were left to bury the remains of an unknown Yankee soldier whose family may never know his final resting place.

The train moved on.

Upon arrival at Montgomery, John learned that they were to be transferred to a steamboat waiting to take them to Selma, Alabama where they would be transferred to a second train that would transport them to Meridian, Mississippi.

After the released prisoners disembarked from their steamboat ride, John and the other former prisoners most likely expected a similar train ride on this leg of the trip as they had taken from Andersonville. Instead, the men were dealt another cruel indignity. The train cars waiting for them were not passenger cars but cars normally used for hauling animals. Never the less, as long as the train was moving away from Andersonville the men were ready to get on board without any hesitation.

After surveying their options some of the men chose to ride on top of the cars rather than share the cramped quarters with the horde of former prisoners who smelled as bad as the lingering stomach-turning odor of animal remnants.

The train ride was not a direct route to Meridian, but required another steamboat ride on the Tombigbee River and a second train to Meridian. Upon their arrival John and the troops were told they would have to walk the rest of the way to Camp Fisk near Vicksburg. The railroad line around the Vicksburg area had been torn up during the war so they were shown the road to Vicksburg and the parole camp and told to start walking.

Chapter 16

Camp Fisk

When the ill and frail John King arrived at Big Black River, he was exhausted and needed help to walk. Then, in typical army fashion, the seriously ill and dying men were not allowed to cross Four Mile Bridge to the camp until they'd received specific orders. During the wait, some of the men spotted a pole sticking up on the horizon and although they were too far away to see any detail they knew it was "their old stars and stripes." They were overwhelmed.

Peter Roselot, born in France on October 28, 1849, was a member of Company E, 50th Ohio Volunteer Infantry and recalled that incredible moment when they first saw the flag.

Camp Fisk, Four Mile Bridge

"We had marched on foot to Big Black River where we beheld the glorious Stars and Stripes once again. We cheered and shouted until hoarse, then we had a square meal of Uncle Sam's gruel and then marched across the bridge and bid farewell to Rebeldom forever." [143]

The parole camp came about when Assistant Adjutant General Captain C.A. Fisk, while stationed at Vicksburg, began receiving requests for food, clothing, and other supplies from a number of Confederate and Union officers in charge of area prisons. Realizing the enormity of the task and the potential cost of packing and shipping everything, Captain Fisk suggested that instead of bringing the supplies to the prisoners, maybe the prisoners should be brought to the supplies. Both sides liked the idea, and a plan was initiated and the construction began. Since Captain Fisk had suggested the idea, the camp was justifiably called Camp Fisk.

The neutral exchange camp was set up four miles outside of Vicksburg where prisoners from both the North and the South came to the camp, were supplied with food, clothing, and medical assistance and then exchanged man-for-man between both sides.

The site was on neutral ground, but controlled by Confederate officers and the supplies and staff were provided by the Union forces. The Union prisoners brought to Camp Fisk were technically still prisoners of war under the control of the Confederacy, but they were being fed, clothed, and guarded by U.S. troops. It was a good plan but not without its problems. Union officers soon realized that they would probably never see a large number of released Southern prisoners and if they did, the trade would amount to receiving weak and incapacitated troops in exchange for healthy Confederate prisoners who could once again join their former units. After some consultation, it was decided that rather than exchange the men, the troops would be paroled. That way, they were still prisoners of war and could not return to the army. Instead they would remain parolees until they received notification of their official exchange. At that point, the men could then return to the army, but few, if any, would choose that option. [144]

While John had been suffering and struggling to stay alive

in Andersonville, his unit, the 9th Indiana, 121st Regiment, had completed their defeat of Hood's army, retreated from Tennessee, and went into winter quarters at Gravelly Springs, Alabama where they stayed from January 16, 1865 to February 6, 1865. Under orders they were then loaded on transports and taken to New Orleans, where they arrived on the 10th of March.

The brigade was then broken up and the 9th Indiana, after turning over their horses, left on a steamer and arrived at Vicksburg on March 25, 1865 and remained there until May 3, 1865. [145]

This placed John's unit in the Camp Fisk area when he and the rest of the tattered groups of Union prisoners began arriving at the exchange point on Big Black River near Vicksburg. It was here that John King received medical attention from a Confederate doctor who had accompanied them on their trek from Andersonville. John was in poor health and his traumatized and starved physical condition caused him to have only partial memory of what occurred during his early time at Camp Fisk.

Captain N.J. Owings and Private Alonzo Githers, both fellow 9th Indiana Cavalry, Company F troopers, who had arrived from New Orleans with John's original unit were at the Camp Fisk site when John and the other debilitated and diseased prisoners arrived. Private Githers had been with John through various skirmishes and was with him when he was captured at Sugar Creek.

The next time Githers saw John was when he staggered into the parole camp. He gave this description of what he witnessed: "John was in a broken down physical condition and complained of and was suffering with what was called scurvy. His legs being much swollen and otherwise bore marks of exposure."

Captain Owings added, "When private King returned to

the command at Vicksburg, Mississippi he was in a deplorable condition, physically suffering with scurvy which he had contracted in prison. He was ragged, dirty, barefooted and otherwise showed marks of cruel treatment and extreme exposure."[146]

John King wasn't the only one glad to see his 9th Indiana friends. Corporal J.A. Brown and the rest of the surviving men from Major Lilly's unit at Sulphur Trestle had also arrived at Vicksburg along with Lieutenant Joseph T. Elliot who had witnessed the starving and skeletal enlisted men as they left the Andersonville prison.

Elliot was an officer and in much better physical shape than the other parolees at Camp Fisk so he received a little special treatment from those in charge. He was allowed to go into the city of Vicksburg.

"After our arrival I got a pass and went into the city and found, to my surprise, that Captain Owens's company of the Ninth Indiana Calvary was stationed there. The boys in that company were nearly all from about Indianapolis, and a better hearted set of men than they never lived. I shall never forget their kindness."

When the Rebs officially handed over John and his companions to U.S. command, the scrawny, sick, and shoeless Yanks felt a glimmer of hope for the first time that they might return to a normal life. The commissary was opened for the troops and a happy, hungry, smiling line of men gorged themselves on hardtack, dried beef, and pickled cabbage.

Private Otto Bardon of Company H, Ohio Volunteer Infantry recalled an incident while in the parole camp. "While we were here we learned of the assassination of President Lincoln by a Rebel. The prisoners became wild with indignation and started for the Rebel headquarters. The Rebel major that had charge of us fled across the

Big Black River bridge for safety until we learned the particulars of the President's death." [147]

Although blankets were provided for the men at the parole camp, there was still no shelter available. Once again, they were forced to build their own huts or sleep on the ground, but this was a minor annoyance since they now had such luxuries as fresh vegetables, a bar of soap, and writing materials for letters to their loved ones. The whole camp was in a state of excitement, they knew that soon they would head north on the Mississippi away from the nightmare of war and on to the fulfillment of their battle-field and prison dreams. [148]

.

Chapter 17

Mismanagement, Miscalculation, and Misconduct

While the Camp Fisk exchange was taking place, Captain Mason and the *Sultana* had left New Orleans and were headed north toward Vicksburg.

From the beginning of the business trade on US rivers, steamboats were built to last only four to five years, using crude and dangerously constructed boilers. Between 1816 and 1860 boiler explosions destroyed 200 steamboats. During that same period, more than 1,500 people had been scalded, crushed, burned, or drowned. When it came to steamboat travel, you bought your ticket and you took your chances.

When Captain Lodwick built the *Sultana*, he installed boilers that were a newer design and different than many of the older boats. The conventional flued boilers were made with eight tubes of varying sizes. Generally, there were four small tubes, three medium tubes, and one large

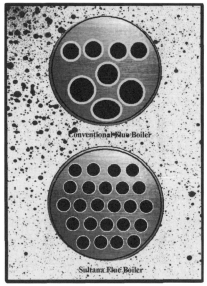

L to R. A conventional boiler and the *Sultana* boilers.

tube. The new flued boilers mounted in the *Sultana* used 24 small tubes for heating the water, but the same rules about wear-and-tear applied to all boats on the river. After only two years in service, ships' boilers were considered old.

As Captain J. Cass Mason piloted the *Sultana* past Baton Rouge and Natchez, he was informed by his engineer that one of the boilers had sprung a leak. Under some conditions the leaks could be repaired while the boat continued its run, but the engineer explained that he could not work on these damaged plates while they were still hot and suggested they make the proper repairs at Vicksburg. [149]

On the *Sultana's* trip downriver from St. Louis, Mason had made a stop at Vicksburg and learned from Chief Quartermaster Colonel Ruben Hatch of the thousands of federal prisoners at Camp Fisk who were to be shipped north in groups of about 1000. When Mason inquired about getting some of the troops aboard the *Sultana* for transport, Hatch led him to believe he could help, although he had no authority in regard to assigning any troops to ships.

Hatch, no doubt, had a plan in which he could profit from this deception. Hatch's history of dishonesty and misconduct in the military had apparently taught him nothing. In his early years of service, Hatch had nearly been court martialed due to a price-fixing scam with the local lumber companies in which he and two other men skimmed the profits and shared the money. During the investigation, it was also learned that Hatch had been selling army supplies to civilians and pocketing the money. He escaped prosecution when his brother, who had ties to Abe Lincoln, bailed him out. After resigning from that post, he moved to a second unit until they discovered he was hiring unqualified employees.

He was sent before an examining board which declared him
"totally unfit to discharge the duties of assistant quartermaster."

Amazingly, he escaped prosecution again and was ordered to
Vicksburg and given the assignment of chief quartermaster.

After arriving at Vicksburg on his way north, Mason wanted to
improve his chances of getting some of the released prisoners. Not
trusting the word of Colonel Hatch he approached General Morgan
Smith, a former steamboat captain himself, in an attempt to secure
a load of troops. [150]

When the *Sultana* docked at Vicksburg, the *Henry Ames* had
already left with the first 1,300 troops, including the emaciated
Eppenetus McIntosh, and another 200 troops had taken off on the
Olive Branch. It seemed likely that the *Sultana* would be chosen as
the next messenger of mercy to take the men home. [151]

This was good news to Captain Mason since the government
was paying five dollars each for enlisted men and ten dollars each
for officers. In the midst of financial problems with his steamboat
business this was certainly a stroke of luck.

While the Mason was pondering the possibility of newfound
wealth, dissension, jealousy, and accusations of bribery surfaced
among officers in charge of the former prisoners. Captain Frederick
Speed had been assigned to assume responsibility of transporting
the troops so after hearing the rumors, Speed made an accusation
of bribery against Captain W.F. Kearns, the assistant quartermaster.
Captain Speed claimed a deal had been made for a kickback with
the Atlantic and Mississippi Steamship Company and he charged
that paroled prisoners were being held until they could be shipped
on packets belonging to that line. Speed had no direct evidence
to support this claim, but whether it was fact or fiction made no

difference. In his mind, someone had made decisions without his approval and was likely guilty of accepting a bribe.

Speed's superior, General Napoleon Dana, other Union officers and Captain Mason became involved and finger pointing, accusations, and denials flew furiously.

One of those involved was the corrupt quartermaster Colonel Ruben Hatch. His involvement in the process should certainly have raised a warning flag but the talks continued with heated words, demands, and threats.

The captains of other boats docked at Vicksburg, including the *Lady Gay* and the *Pauline Carroll*, were nervously awaiting the decision on which boats would get a share of the troops and how many would be assigned to each boat. In the end, Speed agreed to a compromise and it was decided, without anyone in the negotiations knowing the actual number of troops involved, that they would ship all of the remaining prisoners on the *Sultana*. They rationalized that this would be fair since the *Sultana* had a troop and freight contract with the government.[152]

Back at Camp Fisk the order was given for the prisoners to pack up and prepare to leave. With their meager belongings and their intense desire to get home, it didn't take the prisoners long to get ready. For some of the men, one particularly sobering moment occurred when they arrived in Vicksburg and were issued new clothing. John King was one of those overjoyed souls happy to rid himself of the ragged remnants from the prison. The receipt of his new outfit showed up on his military records, stating, "The drawing of clothing at Vicksburg to the amount of $18.27."

Nathan Wintringer, the *Sultana*'s chief engineer, and R.G. Taylor, the local boiler mechanic, completed temporary repairs to the *Sultana*'s leaking boiler. On Captain Mason's instructions, they cut a 26 inch by 11 inch section from the bulging boiler plate and attached a quarter-inch thick plate to patch the leak. The original sheets of the boiler plate were seventeen-forty-eighths of an inch, which was much thicker than the patch. Even though Mr. Taylor disagreed with Mason's plans to make the repair, he stated that while the repair was neither perfect nor permanent, he was satisfied that he had done a good job.

He later said, "Two sheets of steel adjoining the leak should have been taken out, but Captain Mason was eager to move on." Mason decided that any major repairs would have to wait until the boat reached St. Louis and he prepared to accept his cargo of former prisoners. [153]

Captain George Williams was assigned the unenviable task of systematically checking off the passengers as they boarded the *Sultana*. He was working from a list provided by the Confederates that was grossly inaccurate. Some troops began arriving on the wharf by train and others by foot and they became hopelessly mixed as they anxiously waited their turn to board the ship. Williams found it nearly impossible to keep up with the names as the masses boarded and failed to log John King, among many others, as he made his way on board with 351 fellow Indiana Troops.

After he had crammed what he thought was the last of the troops onto the *Sultana*, Captain Williams went on board to make an estimate of how many

Loading troops at Vicksburg

prisoners were on the boat. He made a guess of 1,300 men, basing this number on the two trainloads of men he had seen come to the dock. He was not present when another train had arrived in between those two, so his number was considerably lower than it should have been.

Compounding the miscount was the fact that the actual number of troops on the first two trains was closer to 1,600 than 1,300 and 398 men had been loaded aboard the steamboat before the first train arrived. In addition, a fellow officer told Williams that someone had placed another 650 men on the ship. Without checking any facts, Williams added them to his estimate and somehow came up with 1,966 prisoners.

After checking his addition, he revised the count to 1,866 but that was not counting the number of troops from the uncounted train and any of the prisoners who walked from Camp Fisk. He also did not count the additional passengers (100), the crew (85) or the military guards (21) on the ship, so while the actual number of passengers on board the *Sultana* will never be known, it could have been as many as 2,500 people. [154]

Chapter 18
Hope Becomes Hell

By the time John and the rest of his group were loaded on board, there was hardly a foot of unoccupied space on any of the ship's decks and the jockeying for personal space became a challenge for the troops.

The *Sultana* was built to carry 76 cabin passengers and 300 deck passengers and crewmen. It also had storage space in the hold for cargo and animals. When the *Sultana* pulled out of Vicksburg for her journey north she was carrying approximately 2,100 more passengers than her capacity of 376. The weight on the top deck was so heavy that prior to launch stanchions were installed underneath in order to strengthen the support. But those did little good. The deck was still sagging. [155]

It is believed that there may have been a plan to assign the men from different states to specific areas of the boat but in the confusion of the loading and the mass of humanity this plan, along with others, quickly went by the wayside. It *is* known however that a group of 9th Indiana men had made their way forward and took sole possession of the Texas Deck which was directly in front of the pilothouse.

Sergeant Robert Talkington of Company A of the 9th Indiana Cavalry, desperate for a place to lie down, chose an unusual and creative place for his space and bed for the night. Talkington had heard that there was a dead Union officer on the forward deck, almost over the boiler room. He later said, "I laid down on his coffin using my knapsack for a pillow. I told someone that I was going to hold that officer down for the rest of the night." [156]

On Captain Mason's orders, George Clayton and Second Pilot Edward Ingram steered the boat off the dock and pushed the boat north. Six-foot high white letters spelling out the name *Sultana* were painted on the side wheel. It was a name the men would long remember.

The first day was an exciting one for the troops and they were in a festive mood. John King ran into his friend John Thompson, who also was sent to Andersonville prison after his capture at Spring Hill. As the *Sultana* began its trip up the river, the two men sat on the deck likely sharing their dreams of the future and their memories of the horror they had left behind. [157]

Some of the troops spent their time sightseeing, talking of home and eating their meager, but greatly appreciated rations. The food for the men could have been considerably better but Captain James M. McCowan of Company K, 6th Kentucky Cavalry found that while they had plenty of government-issued rations they couldn't cook any of them because the boat was crammed with troops, leaving no space for a cooking area. As a result, the meals for the men consisted of raw salt pork, hardtack, and bacon.

A few men were issued pickled hog jowls, a step above their prison meals but still very poor-quality meat. Witnessing these hog jowl rations, J.T. Farris of the Indiana Sanitary Commission, who was on board, said, "It will furnish an interesting field of investigation to a faithful Officer to ascertain who pocketed the difference between the value of the pork purchased and the cheap jowls furnished by the conniving unscrupulous Quartermaster." The Chief Quartermaster at Vicksburg was, of course, Colonel Ruben Hatch.

A second problem arose when it was discovered that there was a lack of adequate fluids for the men to drink with their meals so they resorted to washing down the dry rations with water taken directly from the river.

After the meager and putrid meals from Confederate prisons this was like a banquet for them. The parolees ate and talked both among themselves and with the other passengers, sharing their stories of family and their dreams of finally being home. [158]

Down below, the ship's engineer was watching his patched-up boilers with concern and worrying about the overloaded condition of the *Sultana*. To make matters worse the Mississippi was nexperiencing one of the worst spring floods in many years, causing the pilot to search for easy water as the boat pushed upstream.

There was a brief stop the next day at Helena, Arkansas. The city had just experienced an intense rainstorm that had totally flooded the streets but many of the townspeople were anxious to see this strange cargo and the overloaded and tilting boat. The troops were not allowed to leave the boat and the men aboard the *Sultana* were stunned when they saw the citizens of Helena riding in boats down the flooded streets to the dock. One of the locals who made it to the scene was T.W Bankes, a local photographer who set up his camera for a memorable and historically significant photograph of the overcrowded *Sultana*. [159]

That evening, the boat came alive with excitement once again when the men spotted lights from the city of

The Sultana at Helena Arkansas

The *Sultana* at Helena, Arkansas

Memphis, Tennessee. The *Sultana* was scheduled to make a stop at the local docks to unload cargo and replenish their coal supply.

As the *Sultana* docked the men were once again instructed to stay on the boat but the warnings went unheeded by those who were physically able. The men bailed over the side of the boat before it had completely stopped. Many of them spent the evening searching out hot meals at the Soldiers Home but those who had money headed for the local saloons. [160] Some troops, who were strong enough, stayed with the boat and were paid to help unload the ship's cargo of sugar. Fifteen-year-old Stephen Gaston, a musician who enlisted at the age of 13 in Company K of the 9th Indiana, was one of those who chose to work. When his work was done he began stuffing sugar into all of his pockets and every other place he could, including his knapsack and his hat, before heading back to his area in front of the wheelhouse.

Around 10:30 p.m., without any adjustments to the ballast from the loss of the 100 hogsheads of sugar (a hogshead is a barrel-shaped cask), the *Sultana*'s bell signaled the men to return to the boat.

Although the *Henry Ames* had already left Memphis with its load of troops, the skeletal Eppenetus McIntosh had become so engrossed in the civilian surroundings of food, booze, and Memphis music he literally missed the boat. He was still around when the *Sultana* docked and considered himself fortunate when he was able to make his way on board just before the ship prepared to leave. [161]

Shortly after midnight on April 27, 1865, the *Sultana* moved out and stopped at the coal station just across the river at Hopefield Point, Arkansas to replenish its coal before heading north.

Back in Memphis, there were still stragglers who partied too long and missed the boat when it left the Memphis dock. Two were from Indiana: Privates George Downing of the 9th Indiana Cavalry, Company G and James Payne of the 124th Indiana Infantry, Company C.

Payne decided to wait for another boat, but Downing still had a little money in his pocket and paid a man two dollars to row him out to the *Sultana*. Once on board, he told his mates, "If I had not sent home for that money, I would have been left."

Sergeant William Fies of the 64th Ohio Volunteer Infantry and his close friend and fellow Sergeant Asaph Cranmer had claimed spots by the cabin deck near the railing. Just as they were settling down to sleep, Captain Mason made his way from below deck and tried to get to his stateroom. Sergeant Fies later recalled that the deck was so crowded with troops that the captain couldn't find enough room to pass through. Mason was forced to crawl around the men on the outside rail while the men yelled jokes about his awkward and less-than-dignified predicament. [162]

As the overloaded steamer headed north, George Clayton, the pilot, was steering the *Sultana* and fighting the oncoming current, the top-heavy boat, and the dangerously overburdened boilers. He worked his way through a series of islands known locally as the "Hens and Chickens," and then slipped past Tangleman's Landing, cruising at her normal pace of nine to 10 knots. It was 2:00 a.m. when, seven miles down the river in Memphis, they heard the explosion.

The force of the blast was tremendous, nearly splitting the boat in half. The erupting fire cast an ominous glow through the cottonwood trees along the banks of the river and people throughout the countryside felt the earth tremble. Broken boards, pieces of iron, and bodies flew into the air and dropped back onto the deck of the boat with a thundering crash. Hot water and steam from exploding boilers rained down on the shocked and stunned passengers and many people were blown off the boat and into the river.

Those who were not killed outright were scalded, burned, injured, or buried beneath rubble. The blast scattered hot coals from the furnaces throughout the mid-portion of the ship, and the mass of humanity on the boat stampeded for the river.

The *Sultana* Explosion

The *Sultana* had been hugging the shore most of the way to stay out of the strong current, but at this point in the journey she was crossing from one side of the river to the other and was at mid-stream when the explosion occurred. Normally, the river was about a mile wide at Tangleman's Landing but the spring flood had swollen the Mississippi to three times its normal size. Passengers scrambled for the ships life preservers only to realize there were far too few available. Without this safeguard, various parts of the boat became the only hope of those who could not swim. Boards, doors, railings, and anything that would float—including animal carcasses and human bodies—became personal lifeboats.

The frantic passengers rushed to both sides of the boat trampling each other as they ran and jumped *en masse*. The water around the *Sultana* became a sea of bodies, both alive and dead. People were drowning by the hundreds. [163]

No matter how well anyone could swim if they were in this crowd of clawing, grabbing, panicked souls it meant almost certain death. George F. Robinson, a soldier from Company C, 2nd Regiment, Michigan Cavalry, was sleeping between the smoke stacks said, "I did not hear the explosion. I think I was stunned, for the first I recollected I heard someone calling, 'For God's sake, cut the deck, I am burning to death.' Then I tried to find out where I was, and when I did, I found I was in the coal in front of the arches. The deck I had laid on was on top of me. My arms were scalded and the hot steam was so thick I could hardly breathe, and in fact I gave up. My partner, John Corliss, was lying across my legs and was dead, killed by the deck falling on him. I then heard someone say, 'Jack, you can get out this way.' It was some comrade helping his bunkmate out. This is the last I can recollect until someone put his hand on my shoulder and said, 'What will I do? I cannot swim.' I looked around and my God what a sight! There was three or four hundred, all in a solid mass in the water and all trying to get to the top. I guess that nearly all were drowned but that was not the worst sight. The most horrid of all was to see the men fast in the wreck and burning to death. Such screaming and yelling I never heard before or since."

When the explosion woke up James Brady of the 64th Regiment, Ohio Volunteers, Company B, his hair was on fire. He lost most of it before his friends were able to extinguish the fire. He then made his way to the bow of the ship to find some way to save himself. He later told this story: "Oh, what a sight met our gaze! There were some killed in the explosion lying in the bottom of the boat being trampled upon while some were crying and praying. Many were cursing while others were singing, a sight I shall never forget." [164]

Describing his awakening to what seemed like a "discharge of a park of artillery or a railroad collision," Captain J. Walter Elliot of

Company E, 10th Regiment, Indiana Volunteer Infantry found his face, throat, and lungs burning "as if in a boiling cauldron." Racing forward, he found a huge opening in the floor and paused to get his bearings. At that point, he said, "The scene lit up from below disclosing a picture that beggars all description. Mangled, scalded human forms heaped and piled among the burning debris on the lower deck. The cabin, roof, and Texas Deck are cut in twain, the broken planks on either side of the projecting decks. 'Captain will you please help me?' I turned in the direction of the voice so polite, so cool, so calm amid this confusion. There on the last cot on this side of the breach sat a man bruised, cut, scalded in various places, both ankles broken and bones protruding. With his suspenders he had improvised tourniquets for both legs to prevent bleeding to death. 'I am powerless to help you; I can't swim,' I replied, but he answered, 'Throw me in the river is all I ask; I shall burn to death here.' I called to Captain Chapman, and we bore McLoyd aft and threw him overboard." [165]

The emaciated Andersonville skeleton Eppenetus McIntosh was sleeping on the Texas Deck before he woke up in the freezing river. He floated and swam while stripping to his drawers. Looking around he saw other soldiers being pulled under by panicked men so he swam away, preferring to tough it out alone. Exhausted, he eventually found a sandbar where he waited until he was picked up at 10:00 a.m. the next morning by two black men in a small boat.

Fifteen-year-old musician Stephen M. Gaston had eaten two pounds of his hard-earned sugar and then went to sleep with his head against the front of the pilothouse. He woke up while being thrown into the air and dropped back to what was left of the front Texas Deck. One of the huge smokestacks had fallen and crushed the pilothouse directly behind where he had been laying. He was covered with debris and had suffered a serious gash in his thigh. As fire broke out in the remnants of the pilothouse, Gaston knew that despite his injuries he had to escape. One of the fallen smokestack breechings allowed him to slide down to the bow of the boat where he grabbed an empty flour barrel, tossed it overboard, and jumped in after it. [166]

Nathan Williams of Company B, 5th Indiana Cavalry, 90th Regiment was sound asleep when the explosion occurred. Although the upper deck fell on top of him, he was not injured. After climbing out from under the debris he described this scene. "I went forward and caught hold of one of the ropes which was fastened to the bow of the boat; there, I beheld a sight that I never want to be witness of again.

"Men were scalded and burned, some with arms and legs off, and it seemed as if some were coming out of the fire and from under the boiler, and many of them jumping into the river and drowning by squads."

After observing the swarms of struggling and dying men around the boat, and in an effort to help the panicked men, Williams said "I helped throw off everything that was loose letting the men go as fast as they wanted to for many would not listen to reason. But it was not long until I knew I must go, for the fire was getting headway and the boat was swinging around which would bring the fire near me. I succeeded in getting a plank eight feet long and eight inches wide. I held it a short time thinking what was best to do. I soon made up my mind I could swim better with my clothes off, so off they came. Then I threw the plank in and jumped in after it." [167]

A group of men began hacking at the lines that were holding

the gangplank in place in hopes of using it for escape. As the lines broke free the huge board came crashing down killing several men who were standing underneath.

Several 9th Indiana Cavalry troops from Company G and Henry County, Indiana were sleeping on or near the Texas Deck in front of the wheelhouse. Three of them, Corporal William Peacock, Private William C. Hoober and Private Lewis Johnson, were from the same neighborhood in Luray, Indiana. In fact, they had grown up as boys together. A fourth man, Corporal Enoch Nation from nearby Dudley Township, was also with the group. All of them had been captured with Lilly's unit at Sulphur Trestle.

When the boilers blew, the men were jolted awake by the deafening explosion. Private Johnson quickly realized that his neck and shoulders were badly burned, so he got up, walked to the edge of the boat, pulled off his clothes, and jumped into the water. Looking for something to keep him afloat, he spotted some floating timbers on the Arkansas side of the boat and began swimming toward them. He soon realized there were already eight other men clinging to the bobbing makeshift refuge. Much to his relief the men welcomed him aboard and they all hung together as they were carried downriver.

The men were in the water for nearly five hours and some of the men became so cold that they could no longer keep a grip on their makeshift raft and drowned. Johnson was able to hang on until he was rescued by a passing boat. [168]

Ninth Indiana Cavalry Corporal Peacock and Corporal Nation, Company G, were asleep when the ship explosion dropped them into a hole where they were buried beneath a pile of boards and bodies that fell on top of them.

At one time, Peacock had weighed nearly 200 pounds, but his seven months in the Confederate prison had dropped his weight to 91 pounds. His back was bruised, his right hip was badly scalded, and his shoulder was cut and bleeding, but he managed to help others who were buried under the debris. He and Nation helped the dazed and injured men until the fire became so hot that Peacock said, "I had to stop and look out for myself."

William Peacock

Corporal William H. Peacock, 9th Indiana Cavalry

Peacock and Corporal Nation tried to find some escape from the impending doom, but Nation ultimately panicked and ran into the flames and, in Peacock's words, "Was never heard of afterwards."

Peacock climbed to the wheelhouse, which was now crushed and in ruins and looked over the side of the ship at the frightened struggling troops thrashing in the river. He saw that many of the men had not removed their clothes. Some were still wearing overcoats and shoes and quickly sank beneath the freezing water. After shedding some of his clothing, he grabbed a piece of timber, jumped into the river, and began swimming downstream.

After about a mile, he stopped to rest. Someone's hat floated by and he picked it up, put it on his head, and continued to swim downriver. He was eventually picked up by a gunboat just south of Memphis wearing his newly found hat, his drawers, one sock, and a handkerchief tied around his neck.

He was first taken to Fort Pickering, then to Memphis, where he was admitted to the Soldiers Home which had been put into use as a hospital. He spent a day recuperating in the home before being released. Peacock later said, "The explosion was a terrible fatality and the impression made upon my mind by its sufferings and horrors can never be effaced." The last of the group of Henry County boys-William C. Hoover, Private, Company G-went down to a watery grave. His body was never found.

Ninth Indiana Cavalry Sergeant Robert Talkington, who had been sleeping atop the officer's casket, was blown into the river. Dazed and confused, he wandered in and out of consciousness and, believing he was near a small town 12 miles south of Memphis, began yelling for help. To his surprise, someone answered. Floundering in the dark, he heard the sound of oarlocks and the slap of paddles, which he later said "was the best sound I had ever heard." [169]

In addition to the blazing inferno of the *Sultana* and the freezing Mississippi river, there was yet another danger facing the troops. Confederate guerillas were still roaming the area around Memphis and the local Union troops were ordered to shoot first and ask questions later.

The Union sentries were unaware of exactly what had happened upstream and in the darkness and the confusion they began firing at some of the survivors as they drifted by the various guard posts. Other men drifted right by Memphis and were then fired upon by the US Colored 3rd Regiment Heavy Artillery as they floated past Fort Pickering. Eventually the sentries were informed of the tragedy and succeeded in rescuing 76 men from the bitingly cold river. [170]

Two troopers from Lilly's unit, Private William Warner and

John Mooney of Company B, 9th Indiana Cavalry, who had enlisted in Shelby County, Indiana, were sleeping on the cabin deck on top of the side wheel that had been propelling the boat. The blast blew them up in the air and into the river. Private Warner was knocked unconscious but remembered coming up from under the water about a mile from the burning ship.

There were men all around him when he began to swim toward some of the wreckage where a group of panicked men were praying. Just as he reached the men and their lifesaving debris, he spotted a large number of cows swimming toward them.

Fearing that the cattle would overturn their safe haven, he grabbed some loose boards and moved away from the other men. Looking back, he watched as the cattle hit the wreckage and all of the men disappeared beneath the cows and debris. Warner soon found that his underwear was hampering his ability to move, so he took off his drawers and wrapped them around the boards to improve his grip. While battling the freezing water he continued to float down river until a steamer came to his rescue. Nearly unconscious he was dragged on board wearing only his undershirt. The crew took him to the boiler deck to warm him up, gave him a pair of pants, and then dropped him off at Memphis. He was then taken to a local hospital where received a shot of brandy and a hot meal. He was one month shy of his seventeenth birthday. Years later he became the last *Sultana* survivor. [171] He died at the age of 85 on May 18, 1933.

The fire on the *Sultana* was now raging out of control. For those still on board, the choice was clear—take your chance in the river or burn to death. One surviving parolee stated, "The men who were afraid to take to the water could be seen clinging to the sides of the bow of the boat until they were singed off like flies."

The weak and disabled soldiers were begging to be thrown overboard. Several men summoned up their courage and took on the task. M.H. Sprinkle and Billy Lockhart, both from the 102nd Ohio Infantry, threw at least 50 men over the side. [172]

Another compassionate soul was Commodore Smith, a private in the Company F, 18th Michigan Volunteer Infantry. He also tossed many men over the side, and the memory of it was still with him when years later, he wrote, "Do you not think this was a hard task for us to perform? If not, just harken to this moment; Listen to the heart felt prayers of those suffering and wounded comrades and hear the dying requests as they commended their wives, children, fathers, mothers, sisters and brothers to God's kind care and keeping and hear them thanking us for our kindness to them, not withstanding the pain they were suffering."

"They fully realized the fact that their last day, hour and even last minute to live had come; and then to hear the gurgling sounds, the dying groans and see them writhing in the water, and finally see them sink to rise no more until the morning when all shall come forth. Was this not rending to us? My heart even now, after twenty seven years nearly stands still while I write this story." [173]

William A. McFarland of Company A, 42nd Indiana Infantry, another Andersonville prisoner, gave this account of his personal trauma on that frightening and tragic night: "I seemed to be dreaming and could hear someone saying, "There isn't any skin left on their bodies." I awoke with a start, and the next moment the boat was on fire and all was light as day. The wildest confusion followed. "Some sprang into the river at once; others were killed, and I could hear the groans of the dying above the roar of the flames.

I was on the hurricane deck, clear aft. This part of the boat was jammed with men. I saw the pilothouse and hundreds of them sink through the roof into the flames at which juncture I sprang overboard into the river. As I came to the surface of the water, I saw a woman rush out of a state-room in her night clothes with a little child in her arms. In a moment she had fastened a life preserver about its waist and then threw it overboard. The preserver had evidently been fastened on too low for when the little one hit the water it turned wrong end up. The mother rushed into the state room for an instant and was then out and sprang into the water and grabbed the child all of which occurred in the space of a couple of minutes. I swam seven miles down the river and into a drift, where I caught to a log and awaited assistance.

"As day dawned I found that hundreds had followed my example. Imagine my surprise when I observed that woman, whom I had witnessed plunge into the river after her baby, sitting straddle of a log about twenty feet in front of me with the little one before her. We were both picked up by a yawl sent out by the steamer Silver Spray.

After tossing his share of sick and injured soldiers overboard, M.H. Sprinkle took to the river and began swimming. He later wrote of his survival, saying, "I swam over to the west side of the river but the banks were too steep for me so the only alternatives I had was to float down the stream, which I could easily do, or drown. I chose the former but was nearly exhausted.

"On my way down the river I came into contact with two men who were clinging to a trap door about three feet square; neither of them could swim and as I was floating so easily along they begged me to help them get out. I steadied their raft for them and pushed it along down stream. We were getting along fairly well when a drowning man seized my left leg. I tried to kick him loose but failing I let loose of the raft and tried to force him off but could not and was obliged to drag that dead weight until we reached Memphis. We were helped out of the water just above the wharf by citizens and the last I can recollect was they were trying to pry the dead man's grip loose from my leg." [174]

The fire caused by the boiler explosion was now moving quickly toward the stern due to the direction of the wind. As the fire raged the side wheels kept the *Sultana* on course, however when the fire hit and destroyed the side wheels the boat began to turn. Now the wind was coming from the opposite direction and the fire headed for the bow and the mass of humanity who had thought they were safe. It was time to decide whether to jump into the icy river or burn to death. Despite the consequences a few chose not to jump. [175]

Fate played a role in the life of each *Sultana* passenger. William H. Williams of the 18th Michigan Volunteers was luckier than most. When the explosion happened, he was blown into the air and landed in the top of a cottonwood tree. He sat there until he was rescued at daybreak. In contrast, the remains of one person picked up by a ferry boat were so horribly scalded that "not the size of a half dollar of skin was left on the whole body."

A family of seven women and a small child, about seven years old, were on board. Only the fate of the child is known. One of the men working at the wood yard just above Memphis was able to tell the story:

Setting off from the shore in a small skiff, he quickly pulled two people on board. The first was a man with both legs broken below the knee. The second man was missing an arm. Despite the severe injuries, the three of them continued to look for other survivors.

They soon spotted a young girl struggling in the freezing water. She was wearing a life preserver but it was strapped on so low that her head kept going forward, dunking her face-first in the river. They described her as wearing a "fine" night dress and high-heeled gaiters, (spats) that served as a type of boot. As the men tried to grab her, the boat nearly capsized and they missed their chance to save her. She immediately went under and never rose above the water again. [176]

As the frantic battle for life continued up and down the Mississippi the fire on the ship raged on and the *Sultana* finally split in half. Private Hugh Kinser of Company E, 50th Ohio Volunteer Infantry, who was captured at the battle of Franklin, Tennessee and imprisoned at Andersonville, described his eyewitness account of the *Sultana*'s last moments:

"While we were clinging to the tree, we saw in the distance the hull of the *Sultana* come floating down the river with a dozen or more boys still clinging to the burning wreck.

"A mound of earth which had not been overflowed had formed a sort of island and several men from the wreck had floated down and lodged on it. They quickly made a raft of logs and boards and went to their rescue. From our position in the tree, we watched them go, trip after trip, until the last man was rescued. Before they landed with the last man on their return trip, the hull of the *Sultana* went right down, its hot irons sending the hissing water and steam to an immense height." [177]

Later that day, First Sergeant John B. Hinckley of Company A, 9th Indiana Cavalry stood on the banks of the Mississippi to view the site of the explosion. He later said, "We visited the site about ten o'clock. It had sunk in twenty feet of water and the Jackstaff still holding the flag was standing up before the black mass as though mutely mourning over the terrible scene, a silent witness to what it had been. The charred remains of several human bodies were found, crisped and blackened by the fiery element. The scene was sad to contemplate." [178]

By the time the ordeal was over, the death toll had reached nearly 2,500 passengers. The number was staggering. Only about 800 people survived the explosion, and more than 300 of those died later in various hospitals. Many who were not killed outright made it downriver past Memphis before they were picked up, but died soon after from the scalding and burns, long exposure to the water and cold, and sheer exhaustion. Private George Downing of the 9th Indiana Cavalry who had paid for his rowboat trip from Memphis to be on the Sultana died in the explosion.

Captain J. Cass Mason survived the explosion and was seen assisting passengers in the fire and frenzy that followed but he died in the aftermath. His body was never found. [179]

John King woke up at 2:00 p.m. on the wharf at Memphis with an injured back and no recollection of how he got there. Although John had no memory of what took place after the explosion Private Anderson Pinion, the same friend who was captured with John at Sugar Creek, gave this account of what took place between he and John immediately after the explosion: "Me and him was together and he got on a stage plank [used in transferring cargo from a barge to a steamboat] and said for me to not come on the plank or he would drown, so I swam away. I did not see him again until I saw him in Memphis. He said that he had hurt his back while trying to get off the plank to save himself and he was complaining that his back hurt." [180]

While John was suffering and trying to recall what exactly had happened to him the dock area began to overflow with the citizens of Memphis. They had come to see what was going on and wanted to help in any way they could. Ambulances, stretchers, and carriages were making frantic trips between the dock and the various hospitals and homes, which were swamped with victims of the disaster. [181]

During his 16 months of service, John had survived all of his 9th Cavalry battles, being shot and captured at Sugar Creek, the hellhole of Andersonville, and the explosion of the *Sultana*. If he had contemplated his recent run of tragedies, he would have been hard-pressed to see himself as having a string of luck, but he was a fortunate soul, indeed.

The morning after the explosion, a tugboat pulling several small boats headed toward the remains of the *Sultana* to retrieve the bodies still floating or trapped along the river banks. The steamer *Jenny Lind* joined the search cruising the Mississippi searching for and recovering the bloated and disfigured bodies.

New victims came to the surface every day and the boats' crews took on the grim task of retrieving them. Bodies washed ashore up and down the river, some as far south as Helena, Arkansas, nearly 90 miles away. [182]

At the end of each day the boats would return to Memphis with a new load of bloated bodies covering their decks and dump them on a barge anchored mid-river. The search went on for two weeks.

There were fewer than 200 bodies recovered from the river and most were never identified due to a careless mistake by officials in charge of the deceased men.

Originally, the victim's bodies were buried at Elmwood

Cemetery in Memphis, but two years later they were reburied in the city's National Cemetery. When the bodies were exhumed for the reburial the names of the men were written on their coffins in chalk and left overnight for a morning burial. That evening it rained in Memphis, washing the names off all but twenty of the coffins. Approximately 180 of the recovered soldiers were buried in nameless graves. Another blunder and affront to the mistreated former prisoners and unfortunate passengers of the *Sultana*. [183]

The sinking of the *Sultana* is said to be the largest maritime disaster in the history of the United States, but due to the circumstances of the time, few have heard the story.

The nation had been at war for four years, and the news that it was drawing to a close filled the pages of the local papers. April of that year had been a month of crisis. Lee had surrendered to Grant; Lincoln was fatally shot on April 14, and news accounts followed his funeral train from Washington, DC to Springfield, Illinois. General Sherman had just finished off the last battle with the Rebel troops, and John Wilkes Booth had been trapped and shot to death in a Virginia barn. The *Sultana* disaster was virtually ignored by the press. [184]

It is also likely that the military "brass" and the US government tried to minimize the loss of life to cover the negligence of officials in allowing the boat to be so blatantly overloaded.

In April of 1865, three of the Indianapolis newspapers in circulation were the *Indianapolis Daily Journal*, the *Daily State Sentinel*, and the *Indianapolis Daily Evening Gazette*. The *Gazette* was a short-lived newspaper that began publication on December 29, 1862 and lasted until March 9, 1867. The daily four page paper, with no Sunday edition, sold for five cents. The news of the *Sultana* was first published in the *Gazette* on April 29, 1865, two days after the event, which wasn't bad considering the slow communication process, the massive influx of news items, and the confusion of the time. The item was located mid-page on page three of the paper, flanked by ads on both sides.

The story was part of a column on other national news including the proclamation by newly sworn-in President Andrew Johnson that "Thursday, the twenty-fifth of next month [May] was recommended as a day for humiliation and prayer in consequence of the assassination of Abraham Lincoln, late President of the United States."

The *Sultana* story immediately preceded this item and was titled "Terrible Steam Boat Explosion." It was presented as two separate items. The first was the original dispatch and listed the source and date as St. Louis, April 28. It was a two-sentence item. Following the first paragraph, a second story sub-titled "Second Dispatch" listed Memphis, April 28, via Cairo, as the source and date and was four sentences long. There was no other coverage nor were there any follow-up stories in the *Gazette* after the initial article on April 29, 1865. [185]

The *Daily Indiana Sentinel*, another four-page daily, published its first issue on July 21, 1841. It remained under that name until February of 1906, when it merged with the *Indianapolis Star*. The *Sentinel* did not report the *Sultana* disaster until May 2, 1865, five days after the event, but had a little more information than the *Gazette* story that ran on the twenty-ninth of April.

The *Sentinel* also chose to run the story on page three. It was part of a column titled "Telegraphic Dispatches" and then sub-headed "Latest War News." The featured stories included

"Destruction of the Rebel Ram Webb," "The Policy of the New President," and "Progress on the (Lincoln) Funeral Cortege."

Listed under "Interesting Southern News" was a 10-sentence story about the *Sultana* disaster. There was no other coverage, nor were there any follow-up stories after this initial article of May 2, 1865. Some local news items in that May 2 edition of the *Sentinel* included an item of curiosity and others indicative of the time.

City Items

It was a strange coincidence that the same horses that drew the coach that contained Mr. Lincoln when he passed through this city four years ago should draw the funeral car containing his coffin on the 20th.

****

The decorations across Washington Street have been the cause of three or four runaways, and should either be festooned up or else be taken down. They hang so low that they all but reach the heads of the horses, and flapping in the wind scare them.

****

John Turner, Levi Stultz, Jackson Lancerson, Edward Riley and Patrick Dowd were each fined two dollars and costs for being drunk yesterday by the Mayor.[186]

The paper that gave the *Sultana* explosion the best coverage was the *Indianapolis Daily Journal*. This four-page daily paper began June 4, 1823 as the *Western Censor & Emigrant Guide* and then changed its name to the *Indiana Journal* in 1825 before finally settling on the *Indianapolis Daily Journal*. It remained an Indianapolis fixture until it was absorbed by the *Indianapolis Star* in 1904.

The *Sultana* story made page one of the *Journal* in Volume XIV, Number 258 on April 29, 1865. Under a column of headlines titled

"By Telegraph," the top stories were listed as "Johnson Surrenders to Sherman," "Washington Matters," "The Conspiracy and National Affairs," and "The Funeral Cortege at Cleveland."

It also included a double headline that read, "Terrible Steamboat Explosion, Fourteen Hundred Lives Lost." The information in this article was almost identical to the one in the *Daily Evening Gazette* that was buried in the middle of page three in that paper.

The *Indianapolis Daily Journal* was the only paper of the three dailies to do a follow-up story. On April 30, the day following the first article, the *Sultana* again made page one. The three-sentence article gave no information on the particulars of the ship or the explosion, but did update the *Journal*'s readers on the status of the troops. Under a column titled "Postscripts," the *Sultana* was the lead story.

Sultana Disaster

Cairo, April 29.—Some eighty-six of those aboard the ill-fated *Sultana* have been found. The number lost is estimated at 1,500. The Memphis hospitals are full of wounded from the *Sultana*, many being scalded.[187]

Compared to the apparent lack of national coverage of the event, the Indianapolis press's ability to keep the citizens of Indianapolis informed was better than most. Anyone who paid their five cents for a paper would more than likely read everything on all four pages, including the ads. So chances are, those who read one or more of the papers were at least exposed to the *Sultana* story. The question was whether or not it would be something readers retained or discussed when the papers were filled with lengthy articles on the Presidential assassination, the capture and shooting of John Wilkes Booth, the search for conspirators, Lincoln's funeral train, and the last battles of the Civil War.

Although many of the *Sultana* dead went uncounted, over 1,900 troops were confirmed. Indiana logged 352 men, Kentucky had 425, Michigan had 243, Ohio had 460, Tennessee 386, Virginia 50, Missouri 2, and Pennsylvania had 1.[188]

That lone trooper from Pennsylvania was a private in the 13th Pennsylvania in the Union Cavalry. On October 12, 1863, Private Michael Daugherty was involved in a skirmish at Jefferson, Virginia and found himself leading a group of comrades against a hidden Confederate detachment. His leadership and his actions prevented the Confederates from flanking the Union forces, thereby saving 2,500 lives. He was later awarded the Medal of Honor for his actions. Unfortunately, that same day, he and 127 of his fellow troops were captured in a confrontation with an advance unit from General Lee's army. Dougherty and the rest of his cavalry group would spend time in several Rebel prisons before being sent to the brutal and inhumane Andersonville prison.

When Dougherty was released with John King and the other emaciated troops he was a walking skeleton and the only member of his Andersonville unit still living. He made it aboard the *Sultana* and when the boilers exploded he was blown off the boat and into the water. Despite his weakened condition, he was able to swim to a nearby island and was rescued the next morning.

One hundred and twelve of the 352 Indiana troops on the *Sultana* were 9th Indiana Cavalry men, of which 59 were lost, a death rate of nearly 53 percent.[189]

Chapter 19

The Trip Home

Immediately after the explosion, and in the days following, the citizens of Memphis although suffering, beaten down, and impoverished by the war, opened their hearts and their homes to the injured and dying Union troops. They provided food, beds, clothing, and care to men who not too long ago were considered the enemy. The more seriously injured men were sent to local hospitals or the U.S. Government soldiers home which had experienced doctors and staff.

In one of his many post-war affidavits John King said, "The authorities wanted to take me to a hospital at Memphis, but I refused to go to a hospital and I was taken to the soldiers home at Memphis [the Hunt Phelan home] where I was treated about three days by the surgeons whose names were unknown to me and were never known to me. After three days, I was put on a steamer, I think the *Belle of the West* and landed at Cairo, Illinois and took the cars for home." [190] (John was actually put on the *Belle of St. Louis*.)

Hunt Phelan Memphis Soldiers Home, 1865

Captain William S. Friesner from the 58th Ohio Infantry, had been in charge of a small guard unit on the *Sultana and* was now assigned to oversee the transport of about 300 of the survivors, including John King, to Camp Chase in Columbus, Ohio where they would be mustered out. Around 5:00 p.m. on April 29, John and his fellow survivors were loaded on the *Belle of St. Louis* and began moving steadily upriver. [191]

For many of the men, the ride and the impending darkness was a frightening and nerve-wracking experience. The memories of the explosion of the *Sultana* made them recoil in panic at every little noise fearing there would be another explosion. Survivor William McFarland of Company A, 42nd Indiana Infantry, a tinner from Vanderburgh County, Indiana, when confronted with boarding said, "I dreaded getting on a steamboat like a burnt child dreading the fire." [192]

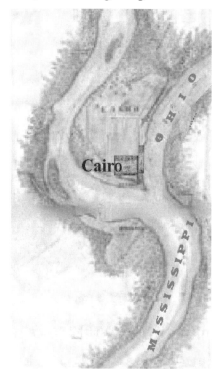

Cairo, Illinois—Mississippi, Ohio River split

The *Belle* reached Cairo, Illinois without incident around 6:00 p.m. on April 30. The men were quickly placed on a train headed north through southern Illinois.

On May 1, the train stopped in Centralia, Illinois, where word of the coming of the *Sultana* survivors preceded them. Citizens of the town turned out *en masse*, offering breakfast and patriotic speeches. Afterward, the troops reboarded the train and proceeded to Mattoon, Illinois, arriving around 2:00 p.m. They were overwhelmed by their reception as the townspeople met them with wagonloads of provisions. John and his fellow survivors were given first-class treatment until the next train arrived to move them a little closer to their official discharge.

The next stop was Terre Haute, Indiana, where the men spent the night before heading to Indianapolis. They were scheduled for a brief stop in the city before heading to the final destination of Columbus, Ohio.

Just two days prior to the Terre Haute stop, in the early morning hours of Sunday, April 30, President Lincoln's funeral train entered the state of Indiana, where he had lived 14 years of his young life in Perry County, Indiana. The train was moving west going through the towns of Richmond, Centerville, Germantown, Cambridge, Knightstown, and Charlottesville, making its way toward Indianapolis. [193]

The nine-car train arrived in Indiana's capital city at 7:00 a.m. on May 1, in the middle of a horrendous rainstorm. Shortly after the train arrived his coffin was unloaded and taken by hearse to the Indiana State House, where it was hurriedly carried inside.

Elaborate ceremonies had been planned for the occasion but had to be cancelled due to the relentless downpour. There would be no grand procession through the streets and Governor Oliver Morton's prepared speech was cancelled.

With no let-up of the

Lincoln Hearse Day 1

Lincoln Hearse, Indianapolis

storm in sight those in charge decided they would devote the entire day to a viewing by the public.

Despite the pouring rain, the crowd was overwhelming. Washington Street became so packed with people that vehicle traffic was impossible. There were so many mourners that people were rushed by the casket with only a brief glimpse of the president's body. After 13 hours the ceremony ended and an estimated 100,000 people had viewed Lincoln's body.

Late that evening, the president's coffin was placed back on the train. With dripping-wet decorative funeral garlands hanging from the train and a fired-up load of steam the train pulled out of Indianapolis and headed to Michigan City, the last scheduled Indiana stop.[194]

The following day, May 2, as the presidential train moved north, John King and the other paroled prisoners arrived in Indianapolis. His hopes, dreams and prayers had been answered. He was home at last.

The men were met by Indiana Governor Oliver Morton and a large gathering of relatives and townspeople who were anxiously waiting for them with a generous meal of bacon and beans and, perhaps trying to make up for the loss of festivities for the deceased

This photo may be a re-creation of the funeral procession that never happened. The photo was apparently taken on May 1, 1865.

president, there were speeches and celebrations throughout the downtown area. Governor Morton, having friends in high places in Washington, DC, used his executive powers to prevent the Indiana troops from being sent on to Camp Chase in Ohio. The ill and injured Indiana troops were instead sent to area hospitals and the healthy ones were allowed to go home. John King was officially discharged from the Army in an individual Muster Out Roll in Indianapolis, Indiana on August 4, 1865.

Nearly 250 Indiana soldiers perished in the *Sultana* disaster; More Indiana soldiers died on the *Sultana* than were killed in any battle involving Indiana Regiments. [195]

Chapter 20

The Last Battle

The last battle of the Civil War occurred on May 12-13, 1865 during the battle of Palmetto Ranch in southern Texas. Despite an informal truce between the Union and Confederate forces, because the war was basically over, Colonel Theodore Harvey Barret ordered the 62nd United States Colored Regiment to initiate what he called a "foraging mission." When the Unit reached the Confederate garrison, the Union troops began confiscating supplies. When word of the Union assault spread, the Confederate cavalry showed up and forced the 62nd to retreat to their camp. Colonel Barret then called for reinforcements and the 34th Indiana Infantry was dispatched from Brazos Santiago, Texas and arrived on May 13. That same day the two units moved out toward Palmetto Ranch to confront the Southern troops. Confederate Colonel John "Rip" Ford was ready for them.

He created a trap that allowed the Union forces to move into the area and then quickly cut off any opportunity for them to retreat. With the Rebs' artillery pounding Barret's troops and their cavalry hitting them on the flanks, it was no contest. Barret ordered his men to retreat. The Southern troops chased them nearly all the way to Brazos Santiago and captured Yankee weapons, equipment, and men, including the color bearer for the 34th and the regimental flag.

During this final action, a Hoosier from Portland, Indiana, Private John Jay Williams of the 34th Indiana, was killed by a sniper's bullet.

He was officially named the last combat casualty in the Civil War.

Private Williams may well have died a needless death. It was later rumored that Colonel Barret had initiated the skirmish simply to further his political ambitions. [196]

From the shot fired over the head of Lieutenant Jefferson C. Davis at Fort Sumter to the death of Private John Jay Williams at Palmetto Ranch, Indiana men played a role in the War between the States from the very beginning to the very end.

Four months prior to that last battle, in January of 1865, Major Eli Lilly was released in a prisoner exchange and was sent to Alabama to resume his military service. Within six months of his release, 83 of his original group of 170 men from the Sulphur Trestle incident were dead. Some died in the battle and others in prison camps or on the *Sultana.* Lilly was later sent to New Orleans, where he was promoted to Colonel just prior to his 27th birthday.

Chapter 21

Post War

Colonel Lilly was stationed at Vicksburg during the prisoner exchange and the loading of the *Sultana* and when the war officially ended he was mustered out in August of 1865. Following his discharge, Lilly returned to Mississippi, settling near Port Gibson, saying that he loved the area with its beautiful wooded landscape and access to the Mississippi River. After settling in, he soon found a business partner, Ceaser Beasley, and the two of them leased a 1,400-acre cotton plantation about 10 miles east of Port Gibson and 18 miles east of the Mississippi River. It did not go well. The story of Lilly's brief and tragic time in Mississippi was later detailed in an article by the *Vicksburg Daily Journal* in 1866.

'Brain illness' kills wife, unborn child of Eli Lilly, Port Gibson plantation owner.

by Judd Hambrick / Special to the Daily Journal

Vicksburg, Miss., Aug. 22, 1866: Emily Lilly, the beloved wife of former Union Army Colonel Eli Lilly, 28, who has the Bowling Green Plantation 10 miles east of Port Gibson, died suddenly Monday at her home from what her doctor calls "congestion of the brain." She was eight months pregnant, so the child was lost, too.

Her doctor said he did everything he could to save both the mother and her unborn boy but to no avail. The entire family has had bouts with malaria for the past several weeks. Colonel Lilly and his 5-year-old son, Josie (Josiah), are totally grief stricken but have recovered from the malaria.

This tragic and untimely death of Mrs. Lilly is just the latest in a series of misfortunes to befall the Lilly family over the past year since they settled in Mississippi from Indiana. Colonel Lilly says it is difficult to believe that he moved onto the Bowling Green Plantation a scant 14 months ago in June 1865. While stationed in Vicksburg at the close of the War, the Colonel thought the area along the Mississippi River was so beautiful and inviting that he decided to stay after the War to build a life for himself and his family.

Since that decision was made, though, he has experienced one devastating disaster after another. The Colonel planted cotton on his 1,400-acre plantation earlier this year, but our current drought hit. His entire cotton crop was ruined.

Then, his business partner, Jesse Beasley, stole all of his business funds and disappeared into this post-Civil War confusion. This summer, malaria struck his entire family. And now, the death of his wife. Total personal destruction right on the heels of him witnessing the death and bloodiness of the Civil War. All Colonel Lilly wanted to do was to build toward a bright future in Mississippi and to forget the dark past of war. What he has gotten, though, is enough to test the patience of Job.

Colonel Lilly is working through some extremely difficult decisions right now. Will he stay on the plantation and make a life in Mississippi? Or will he return to Indiana?
Lilly and his young son buried his wife on the plantation in

a simple ceremony attended by only a few friends.

In the latter part of 1866, bankrupt and alone, Lilly made the decision to move back to Indiana with his 5-year-old son Josie. He returned to his grandparents' home in Greencastle and asked them to care for his son while he went to Indianapolis to look for work. By promoting his prior training as a pharmacist he was able to find work as a chemist with a local wholesale drug house for $40 per month. Over the next 10 years, Lilly worked as a chemist and at a variety of other pharmacy-related jobs, including two partnerships: one in Illinois and another in Indianapolis. Both failed when, once again, he was stung as a result of underhanded dealings by partners.

On March 10, 1876, disappointed and frustrated by the betrayals, the 38-year-old Lilly opened his own small drug shop at 15 West Pearl St. in Indianapolis. In terms of physical space, it may well have been the state's smallest pharmaceutical business. It was 18 feet wide and 40 feet long, similar to many of the "shotgun" houses built during that time period.

Undeterred by the building's size, he hired two employees and, along with his now 14-year-old son Josie, opened the doors.

The business made a respectable $4,000 in its first year of operation leaving Lilly feeling very good about his future, but no one could have dreamed how bright that future would be. [197]

The success of the Van Camp business had already been established and

Eli Lilly and son Josie, first Indianapolis laboratory.

although many sources claim that the Van Camp business had a contract with the army to provide the Union troops with canned pork and beans during the Civil War, it would have been virtually impossible at that time because Gilbert's business was far too small for such a huge undertaking. [198]

America survived a devastating financial, emotional, and physical toll following the War between the States and each state in both the North and South suffered its own personal tragedies. The state of Indiana reported that 24,416 Hoosiers were killed or died during their service, and more than twice that number returned home with disfiguring and debilitating wounds and scars.

When John King arrived home, his family and friends were overjoyed to see him, greeting him with handshakes and hugs, but they were appalled at his physical condition. At some point following his release from Andersonville, the *Sultana* explosion, and his arrival home in Indianapolis, someone took John's picture. His military records show he had been issued $18.27-worth of

John H. King
December 1863

John H. King
April 1865

clothing at Vicksburg following his release from prison, so the photo most likely was taken at Vicksburg following his release from prison and prior to the issue of new clothing.

It's unlikely that John would have been in such bad shape and shoeless following the bountiful train ride home. Whatever the circumstances, suffering from scurvy, malnutrition, dysentery, and a severely weakened body, the bedraggled and shoeless John King posed for the camera to complete a classic "before and after" photo. [199]

Chapter 22

Return to Home Life

Now that he was joyously and finally home with his family, John began the difficult task of trying to regain his strength and health. After many months of rest and a reasonable diet he was eventually able to return to his trade of blacksmithing and the King family, along with other families both North and South, began the process of adjusting to a postwar life.

The military life of Indiana's youngest enlistee, drummer Edward Black, continued following the end of the war as he served beside his father in the 1st Indiana Volunteer Heavy Artillery. In February of 1866 he was finally discharged from service with the rest of his unit. He was now 13 years old.

He died six years later at age 19 and was buried in Crown Hill Cemetery in Indianapolis. His mother kept the drum he had used during the war and many years later his descendants donated the drum to the Indianapolis Children's Museum. [200] By 1867, Gilbert Van Camp had acquired a partner for his growing company. It was now called "Van Camp, Jackson, and Company." Also listed were two employees of the business—Jesse W. Robinson and Charles W. Poston. [201]

John and Katherine now lived in a home at 149 S. Pine Street, which was a little east and south of the downtown area. The U.S. census for 1870 listed the names of Katherine, Wesley, Nettie, and George and contained John's statement that his real estate was valued at $600 and his personal estate was valued at $100.

Most families in the neighborhood did not list a value for their property or estates but John's Prussian-born next door neighbor, 26-year-old George Stumph, listed his occupation as a "Cigar Maker" and valued his real estate at the impressive sum of $2,000 and his personal estate at $200. If this was the true value, the visual comparison of the two homes would have been dramatic.

The following year Wesley, Nettie, and George received a new sister, Daisy, who joined the King family in August of 1871. [202]

While the Kings were celebrating their new home and child and looking toward the future, Gilbert and Hester Van Camp received some devastating news from their family in Franklin County, Indiana. In 1853, Gilbert's parents built a drugstore in downtown Metamora. His father, Charles, ran the business until his death in April of 1861, just as his son's canning business was beginning to grow. Mary, Gilbert's mother, began managing the Metamora business and was still the proprietor on June 2, 1870, nine years after her husband's death.

On that date, Mrs. Van Camp sent an order for some gas burners and a barrel of gasoline to Aldrich and Company in Cincinnati. Since the company had not done business with Mrs. Van Camp before, they contacted Metamora businessman Alfred Blocklege, a local dry goods dealer and regular customer, telling him that if he believed Mrs. Van Camp was a responsible person they would send the order to him and he could deliver the items to her store.

When the gas burners and the barrel of gasoline arrived in mid-July Mr. Blocklege made the delivery and at Mrs. Van Camp's request placed the barrel in the basement of her store.

The use of gasoline at that time was fairly new and consumers knew little about the product. It was generally sold as a cleaning fluid to remove grease stains from clothing and as a treatment against body lice. Because it was so cheap, some people used it as an alternative fuel in their kerosene lamps.

Over the next month, Mrs. Van Camp sold most of the gasoline, but while in the basement on August 9, 1870, she noticed that the barrel had begun to leak. Becoming concerned, she contacted two of her sons, Joseph and Charles C. Van Camp, to help her with moving the barrel and stopping the leak. At around 8:00 that evening her two sons and James Bennenett, a boarder staying in Charles' home, arrived to help.

Also in the store at that time were two children—Clinton Kimble, age eight, and his brother Sheridan Kimble, age five. The boys lived just five houses from the Van Camp store with their mother Angelina Van Camp Kimble, Mary's youngest daughter; their father George, a saloon keeper, and their ten-year-old sister Nora Kimble, who was also known as Ada.

When they were all assembled, Charles Van Camp, Mr. Bennett, Mrs. Van Camp, and her two grandchildren headed down the steps to the cellar while Joseph remained upstairs. Mrs. Van Camp led the way down into the pitch-black cellar carrying a lighted oil lamp.

As the group approached the leaking barrel a huge explosion erupted, blowing out the entire back of the building and one side of the store. The counter, the shelves, the furniture and the store's inventory were virtually destroyed. The remainder of the building immediately caught fire, but the large crowd that had gathered just after hearing the explosion managed to extinguish the blaze. Their quick action saved the remaining framework of the store. Mrs. Van Camp was killed outright, while her son Charles and the two children died within a few days. Mr. Bennett and Joseph Van Camp survived.

Two days later, the Brookville, Indiana paper ran a four-line article on the tragedy, saying only, "Sad Accident: Mrs. Van Camp, a resident of Metamora, was burned to death on Tuesday evening last by the explosion of a gasoline lamp." The building was later rebuilt and is still in use today. [203]

Three years after the Van Camp tragedy John and Katherine King added another family member when their son Forest was born.

Eldest son Wesley had now become a young man and by 1875 Wesley (still living at home) worked as a packer for his uncle Gilbert at the Crescent Packing Company, a subsidiary of the G.C. Van Camp and Son business. Gilbert's son Courtland was the "and Son." The packing business was located at 75 and 77 West Washington Street. [204]

The Van Camp growth took place during the industrialization period for the United States. Following the Civil War, the country's technological, political, and commercial businesses experienced some major changes starting in January of 1870 when plans for the Brooklyn Bridge in New York City were completed.

The following March, the 15th amendment was entered into the United States Constitution, giving Blacks the right to vote. On March 22, 1872, Illinois became the first state to require sexual equality in employment. E. Remington and Sons in Ilion, New York began production of the first practical typewriter on March 1, 1873.

Levi Strauss and Jacob Davis received a US patent for blue jeans with copper rivets in May of 1874. The heavy pants made primarily for miners looked nearly identical as today's Levi's. The price at that time was $13.50 per dozen pairs of pants.

Thomas Edison patented the phonograph in February of 1878,

and in February of 1879, Frank Woolworth opened the first Five–
and Ten-Cent Woolworth store in Utica, New York. That same year,
using a filament of carbonized thread, Thomas Edison tested the
first practical electric light bulb. It lasted thirteen and a half hours
before burning out. In Indiana, the railroad system had grown from
42 miles of track in 1847 to nearly 4,000 miles in the late 1870s. In St.
Josephs, Missouri, the Studebaker brothers of South Bend, Indiana
opened a wagon manufacturing business in response to the hordes
of Pioneers who were heading west to the new open territory. [205]

At this same time, while America was prospering and growing,
John King began feeling the serious long-term effects of his war
time trauma. The debilitating effects of his prison days, the injury
to his back and body from the *Sultana* explosion and the emotional
suffering he had endured began to take their toll.

The scurvy, from which he had suffered greatly, had resulted
in the loss of many of his teeth and had generally impaired his
health and the pain from the injury to his back increased with each
passing year. Looking for any way he could relieve his suffering,
John sought medical help from a Dr. Moore of Indianapolis, but
John was nearly out of funds and was unable to pay the doctor for
his services. The good doctor was kind enough to continue to treat
him, and in return John performed light chores and sawed wood in
an effort to repay Dr. Moore.

Dr. Moore recommended Balsam Copaiba (a stimulant and
diuretic), Sweet Spirits of Nitre (which had many uses, including
the reduction of fevers and respiratory problems) and Allcock's
Plasters to relieve John's suffering.

An advertisement that appeared in the *Indianapolis News* for
Allcock's Plasters stated, "If you suffer from lame back, especially in

the morning, Allcock's Plasters are a sure relief. If you cannot sleep try an Allcock's Plaster well up between shoulder blades—often relieves—sometimes cures. Try this before you resort to opiates. If any of your muscles are lame, joints stiff, feel as if they need oiling, or if you suffer with any local pains or aches, these plasters will cure you."

John tried using the plasters and herbal medicines in search of some relief, but the "snake-oil" unregulated medications available at that time and their fraudulent claims were of no help. With no other options, he continued living life in constant pain. [206]

There was, however, one other source which John sought out. The numbing effect of alcohol. When the plasters, diuretics, and spirits failed, alcohol became his constant source of relief. Unable to work or rid himself of the physical pain and the memories of his days at Andersonville, John, like a great many of the returning troops, continued to drink until he became an alcoholic.

Realizing both his addiction and his dilemma, John began attending local Temperance meetings. The organization held a session on January 18, 1879 at the Temperance Hall on east Washington Street in downtown Indianapolis, and the speaker for the evening was Webster T. Dart, who was born in Indiana but was now living in Iowa with his wife Maria, the city librarian. According to the 1880 census, Mr. Dart was a full-time Temperance lecturer.

He stated his mission as, "Working for the sake of reforming men and raising them up." During his lecture that evening, he told the congregation, "The use of strong drink makes men communists. They think, after having drank their earnings that the world owes them a living and that the man who has taken care of his earnings ought to share them with his more unfortunate fellows—

unfortunate because they have spent their money in the saloons."

Several of the attendees made short speeches. Isaac Davis, district superintendent and a grain merchant from Frankfort, Indiana, gave an account of the work being done by the Temperance people toward Temperance legislation.

Former 9th Cavalryman John H. King was also at that meeting and spoke of "the suffering of some of the men who were trying to reform [including himself]" and how difficult it was for them to get employment, especially from any of the city offices.

"Just as soon as they find that a man has signed the pledge and put on the blue ribbon, they have no use for him."

The Temperance pledge evolved over the years, but the message was always the same, generally stating, "I hereby solemnly promise, God helping me, to abstain from all distilled, fermented, and malt liquors, including wine, beer, and cider, and to employ all proper means to discourage the use of, and traffic in, the use of the same."

The Temperance Blue Ribbon was inspired by a verse in the Bible from Numbers 15:38-39, which says, "Speak unto the children of Israel, and bid them that they make them fringes in the borders of their garments, throughout their generations, and that they put upon the fringe of the borders a ribbon of blue: and it shall be unto you for a fringe, that ye may look upon it, and remember all the commandments of the Lord, and do them."

Each meeting ended with one of their temperance prayers:

Great God! hear thou our prayer tonight, The foes of Temperance may we brave; Guide all our faltering steps aright, Our fellow men from ruin save. [207]

John was still working during this time, but even with his temperance meetings, he spent his remaining time drinking and being drunk. He neglected his family, and his alcoholism, his pain, and his disabilities gave little promise of a stable future.

His lifestyle, the drunkenness, and his unreliability put such a strain on Katherine and their children that by 1880 she and John had separated. Katherine was obviously infuriated and exasperated with her situation and John's failure to be a father and husband.

The Indianapolis city directory for that year read, "King, Kate, widow John H. Residence 51 Peru Avenue." [208]

John may have been staggering and in bad shape, but he was still breathing.

Katherine had born the brunt of John's absence and lack of commitment to the family beginning with his enlistment in 1863. She was left in Indianapolis with three children, a one-room house, an absent husband, and no income. In order to survive, she took in washing from neighbors, friends, acquaintances, and relatives.

Doing laundry at that time was a monumental task. The clothing of the people in those days was worn several days before being washed. The dirty laundry was compounded by the black soot from the coal and wood stoves that heated the homes and polluted the air. It was so bad that the powdery black dust permeated the clothing and stuck to the skin of the city's population.

Katherine King

The physical part of the

washing was backbreaking, involving endless trips to the well for water, which she pumped by hand. Carrying each bucket of water into the house she dumped it in her cooking kettle on the wood-burning stove to be heated.

The wood had to be chopped and the fire constantly tended.

The hot water would then be poured into large tubs for the washing process. As the water became unusable it was carried back out into the yard for disposal and the tubs refilled. A bar of homemade lye soap was used to try and generate some kind of suds while rubbing the soap into the clothing and eventually chafing and splitting her hands and fingers. The next step was the washboard, a small wood frame with grooved metal on both sides of the board where she rubbed the clothes to force the soap into the garment, a process that added more discomfort to her already tender hands and knuckles. Then came the rinsing and drying, dipping the clothes up and down in a tub of clean water and then hand wringing them to squeeze out as much water as possible. The clothes were then hung out to dry on a clothesline in the backyard. During winter and rainy days, they would be hung inside the house.

Once the clothes were dry, the work was still not done. Setting up an ironing board or using the dinner table surface, Katherine alternated between two very heavy and very hot irons. One iron would heat on the stove while the other was being used. She stood for hours on end, ironing and folding and hoping to earn enough to survive. This work and caring for her children was the essence of her days and the pattern of her very difficult life. In her own way, she became another casualty in the "War between the States." [209]

In the early days after his return, John tried his best to lead a normal life, caring for his family and working as a blacksmith at a horse shoeing shop at 120 Fort Wayne Avenue in Indianapolis. John H. Keeper, whose 26-year-old son also worked there, owned the business. John was able to do his job through 1879 but by 1880, when he had reached age 51, his injured back, his scurvy, and his drinking had taken its toll. He was no longer able to perform any sort of manual labor and lost his job. [210]

John was now one among hundreds of thousands of injured, disabled, and the deceased soldiers from the war who had been the foundation of their families but were now unable to properly care for their wives and children.

Because the Civil War pitted the northern part of the country against the southern part, the portion of the population who were disabled or deceased was higher at this time than at any time in America's history. Recognizing the misfortune that would be placed on these families, the US government developed a full-fledged Civil War pension system to aid the men and their families. The amount of each pension depended upon the veteran's military rank and level of disability. Pensions given to widows, orphans, and other dependents of deceased soldiers were always figured at the rate of total disability according to the military rank of their deceased husbands or fathers. By 1873, widows could also receive extra benefits for each dependent child in their care. It was the first program of its kind in America, but the legislators who drew up the plan barred Confederate troops and their families from receiving any benefits. Eventually, individual southern states established their own pensions for disabled or indigent veterans. [211]

Chapter 23

The Paper War

Taking advantage of the pension opportunity, John began corresponding with the US Pension Agency to file a claim for a disability pension. He was now involved in another war, a paper war. It would be nine years before this battle ended.

Since no accurate records had been kept from either Andersonville or the *Sultana,* John had no real proof of how he had suffered while at the prison camp or that he was even aboard the *Sultana* when it exploded because they missed logging his name. The government had to be convinced. John began methodically gathering statements from fellow soldiers who had seen him or been with him during these tragic times and submitted affidavit after affidavit.

Two of the affidavits were from his friend on the *Sultana*, John W. Thompson of Company C, 124th Indiana Volunteers, who following the explosion, had been brought ashore at Fort Pickering. He wrote, "Some of the Gunboat boys gave me some clothing and I walked to Memphis and was placed in General Hospital for a few hours and then went to the Soldiers Home. The next morning after the explosion I saw King on the wharf and he was in a crippled condition. So much so that he could scarcely walk. I saw and chatted with him on the *Sultana* the night of the explosion and know he was on the boat." [212]

Because John King had requested pension money for his

disabilities due to the scurvy and back injury, he was required to follow government procedure and was sent to an examining physician.

Dr. Henry Jameson filed this brief report after completing a physical exam:

"Has lost all front teeth in upper and lower jaws and two molars in each jaw. On the left side, the remaining teeth are all loose. Evidence of former Scorbutus [scurvy]. Disability ½. No evidence of disease of spine but has small pile tumors the size of filberts [a nut cousin to the hazelnut] Disability ¼."

Based on the result of this report, John was awarded a pension of $4.00 a month on August 17, 1882. [213]

While John's life and lifestyle were deteriorating, the Van Camp business continued to grow over the years, starting when Gilbert began packing fruits and vegetables in five-gallon cans to increase his client base. He now sold directly to retail grocers in addition to his regular Fruit House customers. The grocers would open the cans and sell the contents to customers by the pint and quart. Gilbert required the grocers to return the cans when they were empty so they could be recycled.

Gilbert's business was doing so well that in 1882 he added a processing and canning operation at 202-224 W. Market Street. When the new plant opened, Gilbert and Hester's son, Frank, was named Secretary and Treasurer. He was only 20

Gilbert Van Camp

years old but in the years to come he would validate his father's decision. Frank's older brother George Van Camp also worked in the plant as a fruit packer. George married Nancy Jennie Sinks in July of 1879. At the time of their marriage, George was 17 years old and Jennie, the oldest child of Andrew and Catherine Sinks, was 18.

The business grew and ran smoothly until October 3, 1891, when the plant suffered a devastating fire. The Oswego, New York *Palladium* ran an article three days later giving a brief description of the event.

Big fire in Indianapolis

The Van Camp Packing Company's Works Completely Destroyed.

"INDIANAPOLIS, Oct.5, 1891-Yesterday fire completely destroyed the works of the Van Camp Packing Company. The season has been a busy one and the establishment was packed with canned goods, catsup, etc. The total loss will reach $200,000 on which there is $149,000 insurance distributed among eighty companies. Four firemen were caught by a falling wall and badly but not seriously hurt. Fireman Hurley was overcome by the heat and will probably die." [214]

After the fire, the Van Camps pulled themselves together and began rebuilding. It was also around this time that today's world-famous Van Camp Pork and Beans came on the market.

There are many versions of the story detailing how the Van Camps developed the "Pork and Beans with Tomato Sauce" recipe. Some believe that Hester used an old Raymond family recipe as the source for the new product; this theory does have some credibility, since Hester had a major role in the early development of the business.

Most sources credit the Van Camps' son Frank as the source of the groundbreaking new recipe.

There are several versions of the story about how he came up with the idea, and all claim it was an accident. A preferred version has Frank bringing his lunch to work everyday during the rebuilding period to save time and money as he worked to salvage the family business.

One day a client delivered a load of plain baked beans to the Van Camp facility to be reprocessed. It happened to be lunchtime and Frank decided to open a can of the beans as part of his lunch. His first bite found the beans to be overly dry and bland so he decided to add a little seasoning. He opened a bottle of Van Camp's catsup and poured it on the beans. He really liked the taste.

At that time baked beans had been baked mostly in molasses but with some experimenting and tasting trials, Van Camp's Pork and Beans with Tomato Sauce was created. It became the company's most successful product and launched the Van Camp business into international markets. [215]

While the Van Camp business was flourishing, John King, not satisfied with his four-dollar monthly income, made the year of 1883 a busy one for the Pension Agency. He bombarded them with general affidavits seeking an increase in his allotment.

He began working with Indianapolis attorney C.H. McCarty, who prepared and submitted the affidavits and had county clerk Moses G. McClain notarize them. Mr. McCarty usually charged a 10 dollar fee for this service, but it must have been apparent that John didn't even have 10 cents because he decided to wave his fee. He noted on each document that there would be no payment. [216]

Clerk McClain used his stamp and his signature on May 5, May 14, May 28, and April 17 of 1883 as witness to John's signature as he inundated the agency with documents. By September 26, 1883, the

Pension Agency had either been convinced, or they surrendered, and John received a two-dollar increase, bringing his monthly income to six dollars. John took a break and the agency received a rest.

In 1884 John did not file any new requests for an increase. In 1885, John and attorney McCarty filed for and received a review of his pension records and the evidence of his ongoing back problems. The agency verified that John had had no pensionable disability payments from his spine injury since his first grant on August 17, 1882, but the agency's Medical Referee, John Campbell, responded by rejecting any increase for the back injury. [217]

In December of 1886, John was living at the Grand Hotel in Indianapolis which was located at 109 South Illinois at the intersection of Illinois and Maryland Streets. The hotel had been built in the early 1850s and was originally known as the Morton House. After the change in ownership and some renovation it now offered 250 rooms and claimed to be fabulously furnished.

It became a favorite stopping place for commercial travelers who paid from three to five dollars a day for a room.

Special features included steam heat, electric lighting, artificial and natural gas, a large public dining room, a private dining room, and a club room. The hotel offices, a writing room, and the lobby occupied the first floor. Other services included electric bells, communicators, telegraph, and typewriter offices.

The building was six stories high and had a basement entrance which led

Grand Hotel, Indianapolis

to the Turkish baths, a bar, and a billiard room.

That is where John resided, not in the elegant hotel. [218] The cheap rent and the in-house bar most likely influenced his decision.

Using the hotel office facilities, John began writing to the Pension Agency asking for additional pension money for his back injury and further compensation for his health problems due to the scurvy. He petitioned to upgrade his pension to sixteen dollars a month, stating that, "He is now greatly disabled on account of said results of scurvy and asks pension commensurate with his degree of disability." [219]

As a result, the Pension Agency required John to have another examination, this time by the Board of Pension Surgeons at Danville, Indiana. Doctors O.B. Johnson (president), T.W. Johnson (secretary), and I.N. Brent (treasurer) were the board-certified physicians who examined John and gave the following report:

"Gums spongy, tongue pale and flabby, six teeth remaining lower jaw, five teeth remaining upper jaw. Considerable absorption (decomposition) of alveolar procipes (tooth sockets). Pain in lumbar spine, liver enlarged, skin and coripuictinae (second layer of skin) yellowish. Spleen and lungs normal. Soreness in epigast (stomach area), patellar (knee bone), tendon reflex, heart murmur. Hyperauxesis (swelling) with lower limbs.

Disability exists equal to ¾. Disease of gums, loss of teeth are legitimate results of scurvy.

Applicant has been very interdependent in use of alcoholic liquors and of course the results are apparent in the nervous system. Hence rating is made very low and is not intended to cover results of vicarious habits." [220]

John was highly displeased with the results of the response by the Pension Agency medical board. Even with the gruesome descriptions and severe health issues the Agency had turned him down, again denying his request for an increase. He then wrote another sworn affidavit to the Pension Agency, claiming, "Great injustice was done me by the Board of Pension Surgeons at Danville in their report of any alleged examination on April 20, 1887 and for the purpose of receiving exact justice now respectfully appeal to the decision of some other board of surgeons. At the time of the alleged examination only one of the surgeons said anything or examined me and he did not make a thorough examination. "He blindfolded me, laid me on a lounge and looked in my mouth. Also, I ask allowance of pension on account of spinal injury alleged in my original declaration. I am unable to follow my occupation as that of blacksmith and having no other occupation I am unable to earn my subsistence." [221]

Around that same time in 1877, while John was suffering and struggling with government red tape the Indiana General Assembly passed a bill authorizing the construction of a monument to honor Indiana veterans who participated in the Civil War.

An earlier attempt at a monument began in 1875, but did not materialize. With a new grant of $200,000 a committee was appointed and instructed to build a monument on a downtown area known as Circle Park.

The committee began by holding an international competition to find an architect to create a design for the monument. Architects from leading cities around the world submitted 70 creative and exceptional designs. One of those entries came from Indianapolis architect Adolph Scherrer, a Swiss-German architect who designed several Indianapolis buildings, including the City Hospital and the Elks Club building. Scherrer lived at 87 Union Street and was partnered with W. Scott Moore. They had offices at 5 and 6 Claypool Block, on the northeast corner of Washington and Illinois streets.

As the submissions began arriving each was assigned a random number, allowing the judges to make their decision only by number and not by name. The board eventually chose design number four, a towering obelisk with magnificent sculptures and fountains. The winner was Bruno Schmitz of Berlin, Germany.

When the cornerstone was put in place on August 22, 1889, it contained a list of all the soldiers from Indiana who fought in the war on behalf of the Union. A photograph of Schmitz was also included.

The cornerstone read

August 22, 1889

ERECTED BY THE PEOPLE OF INDIANA

Act of General Assembly March 3, 1887

It took 12 years to complete the project with a cost of approximately $600,000. The monument was officially dedicated with a full ceremony on May 15, 1902.[222]

On June 13, 1888, John finally received a pension increase.

His monthly allotment went from six dollars a month to 16 dollars a month following a physicians' report from yet another board of surgeons. This report included the opinions of Indianapolis doctors R.F. Stone and C.E. Wright. The physicians' report was straightforward, specific, and uncomfortable to read.

The doctors declared that John had a loss of teeth due to scurvy and that he had constant pain, weakness, and stiffness in the small of his back. He showed an inability to hold his urine and was often unable to have an action from his bowels, all of which was attributed to injury in the service.

He had only five teeth in the upper jaw and six teeth in the lower jaw, and these were not healthy. His skin was healthy, though his muscles were somewhat flaccid. They found no decided delineation and his complexion was florid (having intense color). The report stated that he had sour belching and no doubt suffered from some indigestion from his loss of teeth. His body inclined forward at a 15-degree angle and a normal erect position was apparently impossible.

They also stated that stooping was apparently very difficult and painful for John and his erector spinal muscles and lumbar region were rigid and painful to pressure. His glutant muscles were flaccid, they reported, and one-third atrophied. There was no sciatica or tenderness. The results were that another affidavit was received and another affidavit rejected.[223]

At the same time John was busy grinding out affidavits, U.S. Senator Benjamin Harrison from Indiana was busy running for president. He had received the Republican nomination to run for the Presidency of the United States in August of 1888.

Harrison, the grandson of former President William Henry Harrison, moved to Indiana from Ohio in 1854 to begin a law practice and soon after became active in the Republican Party.

In 1862, he answered the call of President Lincoln and Governor Morton and enlisted in the 70th Regiment of Indiana Volunteers as a colonel. During his three years of distinguished service, he was promoted to brigadier general. When he left the military at the end of the war, he resumed his law practice before entering the United States Senate.

In 1888, his name was submitted to the Republican National Convention as the Republican Party candidate for president by the

Indiana delegation. On his acceptance by the delegation, he began an active role in his campaign, making a great many speeches and appearances with his running mate, Levi Morton from the state of New York.

Morton, who as a boy worked in a small country store, became a wealthy and influential banker and was highly respected in the Republican party. Harrison's opponent was incumbent President Grover Cleveland.

It was a close campaign in which Cleveland won the popular vote but failed to carry his home state of New York. He lost to Harrison in the Electoral College. [224]

While President Benjamin Harrison was acclimating himself to his distinguished role, in October of 1889 John King had not given up and was still trying to strengthen his case for a larger pension. He persuaded his friends Seth Green and Michael W. Nye to file an affidavit to the Board of Pensions on his behalf.

In his statement, Mr. Nye wrote, "I first knew said John King while he was in the army in camp at Indianapolis, Ind. and at my house. At that time he was sound and able bodied to all appearances. I did not see him after he left the city of Indianapolis for the field with the regiment until about April 1865 when he came home from the army. I saw him within a few days of his return. He was then very lame in his back or spine and it was with great difficulty that he could walk and he told me then that his back was injured while upon the steamer Sultana by its explosion when he was on his way home from rebel prisons.

I make a liniment and I have often given the liniment to him and rubbed his back and spine with it ever since he came out of the army. I never made any charge for the services or medicine."

Seth Green of the 9th Indiana Cavalry, Company K. was also a survivor of the *Sultana* and lived in Carmel, Indiana. He was drawing a pension for head and neck scalds.

After the war, Seth tried to help his fellow cavalryman by frequently allowing John to stay at his home and paying him for whatever work John was able to do. He also bought plasters for John "to allay the pain and misery he suffers in his back."

In 1891, John sought help from Dr. Darius Purman. The doctor had been living in Phoenix, Arizona but returned to Indiana with his wife Mary and sixteen-year-old son Thomas, both of whom were born in Indiana. The family was living at 24 Gregg Street along with John Moore, a boarder, and Rore Ray, a female Black servant. The doctor's office was at 186 ½ Fort Wayne Avenue.

In the doctor's September statement on a government form titled "Medical Evidence," he wrote, "I was first consulted by John H. King about March 1st of 1891. He was then and still is suffering from an injury to the lower part of his spine. There is a deformity of the vertebrae caused by an injury (so he tells me) received when the *Sultana* steamer exploded on the Mississippi River April, 1865 when returning from 'Petrol [Parole] Camp' [at] Vicksburg. He can hardly get about because of the pain he consistently suffers. He has not been able to perform **any** manual labor since I first began treating him last March." [225]

When affidavits were filed with the Pension Agency it was normal procedure to occasionally send letters to officials in each city where the claim originated asking that they verify the credibility of the person giving the statement. Apparently the only official in the area of John Thompson's home of Fishers Switch, Indiana was Harry Fisher. Mr. Fisher was in charge of the railroad switching stationand he penned this reply to the agency saying,

Fishers Switch Yard. 11/25/89

"The witness name John W. Thompson stands fair in the community as 'fair' as I know." [226]

Chapter 24

Sledgehammer King

After a period of living on his own, relying on his friends and struggling to survive on his meager pension, John realized that it couldn't last and was forced to find a way to provide himself with some sort of income. He decided to begin giving public lectures, choosing his personal war experiences and Temperance as his topics. The lectures were free but John always passed the hat for donations at the end of his program. He would then take the proceeds from his lecture and head for the nearest saloon.

Apparently the lectures were rather successful. He adopted the name of Sledgehammer King and had a series of posters printed proclaiming himself to be "A wonderfully gifted orator."

He began traveling outside of the Indianapolis area to give his lectures, venturing into adjoining states when he could find an audience. While in Paxton, Illinois giving one of his lectures, John became ill and was bedfast nearly three days while being treated by the local doctor.

J.H. King original poster

He stated in one of his affidavits that, "Mostly I have used the remedies of Dr. Moore and having but little means I could not pay for skilled medical services. I rely mostly on the plasters but usually I am without hope and do not believe anyone can do me much good except to partially deaden the pains."

His back pain became constant and so severe he was not able to sleep in a bed. Eventually he was forced to settle for a reclining chair that allowed him a few restful hours. [227]

While battling his ill health and constant pain John continued to travel and lecture whenever and wherever he could. He enlisted the aid of friends and acquaintances to locate a church, a revival, or a Temperance meeting where he could speak.

Samuel Sawyer, a minister from Indianapolis, became friends with John and agreed to aid him in acquiring speaking engagements. Reverend Sawyer, a graduate of both Princeton and the Union Theological Seminary, was well-known in Indianapolis and had an interesting and varied career. While serving as the chaplain in the Forty-Seventh Indiana Volunteer Infantry, he was in Memphis when the city was captured by Union forces on June 6, 1862. After the battle, General William Tecumseh Sherman wanted to keep the Memphis newspaper, *Appeal,* in operation in an attempt to generate goodwill among the people of the southern city and selected Reverend Sawyer to be the paper's editor. General Sherman also wanted to improve the character of the newspaper so he was a regular visitor to the office to consult with and counsel Reverend Sawyer. After a year, Chaplain Sawyer left the paper when he was appointed as commissioner to lease abandoned plantations in Arkansas, Alabama, and Louisiana.

When the war was over, Sawyer remained in Tennessee and

became the president of a school in the eastern part of the state. From there, he returned to the ministry by becoming the pastor of a Presbyterian church in East St. Louis and then moved on to another church in New Jersey. Around 1882, he returned to Indianapolis as pastor of the Eleventh Presbyterian Church. Despite his abilities and reputation, Reverend Sawyer was not a wealthy man. In fact, he lived most of his life in a state of near poverty.

Perhaps his understanding of hardship and his role as a minister were the reasons he so willingly assisted the equally destitute John King. [228]

Reverend Sawyer was very aware of John's many problems. His kidney failure, the injured back, his inability to do any kind of manual labor, the alcoholism and the lack of a consistent income.

The minister lived and worked in Room 5 at the Abbett Building at 31 1/2 Virginia Avenue in Indianapolis. To help his friend, the reverend offered to write a postcard to a fellow minister in Ambia, Indiana requesting permission for John to speak to his congregation.

He received a reply on the letterhead of the Golden and Bartlett Phoenix Insurance Company of Brooklyn, Indiana saying,

"Dear Sir:

Your card speaking of your friend who would like to come here and lecture on temperance is received. Would say that I am sorry that we cannot have him come here. Our minister and family are sick with scarlet fever and many others are sick also.
Yours truly, W.L. Bartlett." [229]

Throughout his speaking engagements and traveling, and

despite his health issues, John remained steadfast in his quest for an increase in his pension.

On September 3, 1890, John underwent another exam by the board of surgeons in Noblesville, Indiana. Doctors A.R. Lucke, W.B. Graham, and H.E. Davenport returned this report to the Pension Agency:

"Nutrition fair. Tongue red and fissured, throat congested, right chest wall larger than left, dry bronchial sounds in upper lobe of both lungs, chronic bronchitis exists. Area of dullness over heart, 2 in. increase. Action very irregular, intermittent and weak. Loss of one beat in five. Apex (lowest point of the heart) beat normal in location. Mitral (Heart valve) regurgitation present.

"Spine tender on pressure. Loss of suration (definition) along the spine. Asthesiometer (Measures corneal sensitivity) Three inches parted. Right thigh more normal in sensation. Capsulitis (Frozen joint) in left shoulder and elbow. Deficient motion in left leg and arm. Deficient grip in left hand.

"Teeth all gone except for a few old sharp gums absorbed and spongy. There are scorbutis (Scurvy) lesions on inside of cheeks. Occasional difficulty in urinating from enlarged prostate.

We consider the claimant a physical wreck."

That report got John another dollar a month. He was now up to 17 dollars a month. [230]

Over the years as John's health continued to decline, and his income was at or below the poverty level, the Van Camp business continued to grow. By 1890, the Van Camps had three thriving businesses.

The Van Camp Canning Company, which was a fruit packing plant, had Gilbert as president and his third child, Frank, as secretary and treasurer. The company was located at 300–400

Kentucky Avenue, and if you wanted to contact the business by phone, the number was 816. Gilbert and Frank each held those same titles at their Van Camp Preserving Company which listed their product as fruit, butters, and preserves while doing business from the same Kentucky Avenue facilities.

Gilbert's eldest son, Courtland, had now started his own company. It was a hardware business, possibly following in the footsteps of Hester's brother and Courtland's uncle, John Raymond, in Greensburg, Indiana. The business was a wholesale hardware store that also offered iron products. It was located at 78–82 South Illinois Street.

Courtland began his business in 1876 with J.A. Hanson and minor partner D.C. Bergundthal selling blacksmith supplies, general store goods, and hardware. The company was called Hanson-Van Camp until 1888 when it became Van Camp Hardware & Iron Company and expanded its inventory to include tinners' supplies, woodwork for carriages, and wagons, and guns. [231]

Courtland was now competing against a solidly established German-immigrant hardware entrepreneur by the name of Clemens Vonnegut, who was a Hoosier-native and author Kurt Vonnegut's great-grandfather.

Vonnegut had been a salesman for a textile firm in Amsterdam, Holland before coming to Indianapolis in 1851 and in just two years he became a respected member of the city's business community when he established the Vonnegut Hardware Company on East Washington Street.

In those early days, Clemons partnered with Charles Volmer, a fellow immigrant, in a merchandise business called Volmer and Vonnegut. Volmer later set out to explore opportunities in the

West and was never heard from again, making Vonnegut the sole proprietor of the business. Charles eventually changed the name to The Vonnegut Hardware Company. Van Camp and Vonnegut would be successful businessmen and friends for many years. [232]

On November 5, 1891, one year and one month after John's last pension increase, he had not yet conceded his paper battle with the Pension Agency—he was ready to give it at least one more try. After filing a new request he was told to appear before doctors S.H. Mapes and J.J. Yawn, members of the Indianapolis Board of Surgeons. The Pension Agency, the members of which must have known John rather well by this time, received a report from this board regarding the latest examination that added to the mystery of the coming and going of John's teeth and other serious health issues mentioned in prior reports.

> *"Teeth all absent from upper jaw, all gone but three from lower jaw. Tongue red but not fissured. No curvature of the spine, no Cicatrisantia (Scar) or other external marks of injury to spine.*
>
> *"Coordination slightly impaired, reflexes normal. Claimant is anemic and seems feeble. Walks with an unsteady gait and seems much debilitated. "There is no spine lesion but claimant has severe lumbago as evidenced by pain and tenderness over lumbar region.*
>
> *"Inability to stoop over and touch fingers to the floor, also unable to lie straight out upon the table and flexing of either thigh upon abdomen is limited about one half. Heart's action and position normal, rhythm irregular. No valve murmur or evidence of organic lesion.*
>
> *"Claimant is known by every member of the Board to have*

been what is known as a hard drinker and how far the results of this may be a factor in the condition of his diseases we are unable to determine, but he seems very liberally pensioned." [233]

Blatantly overlooking the fact that John's spine could have been damaged without external scars, the report was the end of any hope for additional increases and the end of John's battle with the Pension Agency.

John continued his destructive pattern of being jobless, lecturing, and drinking until he reached a point that his health and his income would no longer allow him to exist on his own.

He was now living on his pension of 17 dollars a month, plus whatever he earned from his lectures, but his drinking kept him broke. Without funds and in ill health, he needed a place to stay that could solve both of these problems.

On one of his speaking trips, he passed through Marion, Indiana and noticed the National Home for Disabled Veterans. The home was relatively new, having been built in 1890.

It was a 151-acre site with barracks, dining hall, administration buildings, hospital, chapel, canteen, a dairy and a working farm, a theater, and a cemetery. Out of money, out of hope and out of options, John applied to the home and was admitted on September 3, 1892.

National Home for Disabled Veterans, Marion, Indiana

While John was at the Home he continued to travel and lecture when the opportunity arose. He kept in touch with his family by occasionally writing letters and sometimes visiting when he was in Indianapolis to give a lecture.

In a letter he wrote to his granddaughter Cora Adams, daughter of Nettie, he exposed his political preference by saying,

"We had a snow last night but it was a Demmocrat snow or it might have staid on awhile. It left us mud like the Demmocrats will leave us to clean up when they are snowed under the next time."

He also told her about a dog at the home and described a meal served by the staff at the soldiers home, telling her,

"We have a dog here we call him Bum as he is pretty good to bum his living. When he first come here he was standing by the cannon when they shot it off. It nearly scared him to death. Now when the drum beats for to put up the flag he always runs for the seller to hide until after the cannon fires as it does both night and morning. You would laugh to see him skadadle just as soon as the drum beats. Sometimes you could see him braking for the seller about the time for he knows.

Dining area, National Home for Disabled Veterans

"Jest from dinner. We had good coffee, bread and butter, green dried peas, potatoes with the hull on them, then pickles, meet. Yes, ram, lamb, sheep meet and mutton. Old Bum the dog will have to be content with sheep bones." [234]

Even though he wrote letters to his family occasionally the responses to his letters were few and far between. Each time he wrote he passionately asked that they write back to him but apparently his alcoholic past was still with him. The wounds he inflicted because of his excessive drinking were too deep, and forgiveness was yet to be found.

After only six months, John left the soldiers home on March 10, 1893 with $49.95 in his pension account. It was his decision to leave. In spite of the Temperance services provided by the facility his drinking had continued. His Soldiers Home discharge papers named his youngest daughter Daisy as his nearest relative, although Katherine and his other children were still living. Based upon the doctors' reports, it was absolutely remarkable that he was still living.

Soon after leaving the home and returning to Indianapolis his health began to quickly deteriorate. It was now spring in Indiana and new life was beginning for Mother Nature, but John King's life was drawing to a close. On Saturday, May 22, 1893, less than eight weeks

John H. King

after he left the soldiers home, John Henry King died of acute alcohol poisoning.

He is buried in Indianapolis, Indiana at Crown Hill Cemetery, section 7, grave number 1427. He was buried in a pauper's grave without a tombstone. [235]

After living on his own, at hotels, with friends, or at the soldiers home, his place of death was listed as 149 S. Pine Street, Indianapolis, Indiana. He had not lived at that address since he was still with Katherine and his children.

Although Katherine's life was not as she may have dreamed and her years with John were filled with anguish and disappointments, as her death drew near she apparently understood that John was unable to overcome his suffering from the scurvy, his injured back, his memories of Andersonville, and the resulting alcoholism.

Katherine died March 20, 1915 and was also buried at Crown Hill Cemetery, section 54, lot 288. Her tombstone is engraved, "Katherine Wife of John H. King." [236]

Some 40 years after John's death, Raymond James Smith, John King's great-grandson, the son of his granddaughter Cora, kept a diary as he lay in his sick bed in Sunnyside Tuberculosis Sanitarium on the east side of Indianapolis. Although he would live many years after the removal of one of his lungs and his 10-year stay at the facility, during an emotional moment as he contemplated his life, he wrote,

Katherine King's tombstone.
Crown Hill Cemetery.

"Fate is a sculptor who shapes the lives of men and destiny is the finished work of fate. At times fate works with beautiful grace but again he molds like a demon of hate. In a way I believe in predestination. We cannot know the purpose of our individual lives but all that befalls us is for that purpose. We can not know the whys and wherefores but I live on to see if I can understand." [237]

Raymond could have written those same words about the life of his great-grandfather John H. King.

Fate may have made John King's destiny far more difficult than most, but even through his many misfortunes and his poor life choices he remained a survivor, and in the end there was understanding and forgiveness.

The Burning of the *Sultana*
By William H. Norton Company C, 115ᵗʰ Ohio
A Sultana Survivor

Midnight's dreary hour has passed,
The mists of night are falling fast,
Sultana sounds her farewell blast,
And braves the mighty stream.
The swollen river's banks o'er flow,
The leaden clouds are hanging low,
And veil the stars' bright silver glow,
And darkness reigns supreme.

Her engines fires now brighter burn,
Her mammoth wheels now faster turn,
Her dipping paddles lightly spurn,
The rivers' foaming crest;
And drowsy Memphis lost to sight,
Now fainter shows her beacon light,
As *Sultana*, steams in the dead of night,
And the union soldiers rest.

The sleeping soldiers dream of home,
To them the long sought day had come,
No more in prison pens to moan,
Or guarded by the gray;
At last the changing fates of war,
Had sprung their prison gates ajar,
And laurel wreaths from the north afar,
Await their crowning day.

For peace has raised her magic hand,
The stars and stripes wave o'er the land,
The conquered foemen now disband,
As melts the morning dew.
And mothers wear their wonted smile,
And aged sires the hours beguile,
And plighted love awaits the while,
The coming of the blue.

On sails the steamer through the gloom,
On sleep the soldiers to their doom,
And death's dark angel, Oh too soon
Calls the muster roll.
A burst, a crash and timbers fly,
And flame and steam leap to the sky,
And men awakened, but to die,
Command to God their souls.

Out from the flames encircling fold,
Like a mighty rush of warriors bold,
They leap to the river, dark and cold,
And search for the hidden shore.
In the cabins, and pinioned there,
Amid the smoke and fire and glare,
The awful wail of death's despair,
Is heard above the roar.

Out on the rivers rolling tide,
Out from the steamers burning side,

Out where the circle is growing wide,

They battle with the waves.

And drowning men each other clasp,

And writhing in death's closing grasp,

They struggle bravely, but at last,

Sink to their watery graves.

Oh! For the stars bright silver light!

Oh! For a moon to dispel the night!

Oh! For the hand that should guide aright

The way to the distant land.

Clinging to driftwood and floating down,

Caught in the eddies and whirling around,

Washed to the flooded banks are found,

The survivors of that band. [238]

Afterword

The responsibility for the *Sultana* disaster ultimately lies within two areas: First, who and or what was responsible for the explosion? Second, who was answerable for the blatant overcrowding of the boat?

Explosion

Early on, sabotage was considered as a possibility for the explosion of the *Sultana*. Sabotage of boats, trains, train tracks, and even buildings was a known method of Confederate warfare. There was speculation that a bomb was camouflaged as coal and hidden in the coal fuel pile of the *Sultana*. It was assumed that the explosive was then shoveled into the furnaces heating the boilers.

There was also speculation that an artillery shell had hit the ship, but after reviewing some very questionable physical evidence and a couple of confessions to altered facts, two separate military investigations gave no credence to either of those theories.

The most convincing evidence indicates that the explosion of the *Sultana* was the result of incompetence by the *Sultana* crew. This conclusion comes from J.J. Witzig, supervising inspector of steamboats for the St. Louis district. In a report by Witzig, he focused his attention on the boiler repairs done at Vicksburg.

He stated that the difference in the thickness of the patch and that of the original iron for the boiler was critical. The normal pressure for the boiler was 145 pounds per square inch, but the patch reduced the acceptable pressure to 100.43 pounds per square inch.

Since the *Sultana*'s boilers carried the normal 145 pounds per square inch from Vicksburg to Memphis, Witzig concluded that the extra pressure was too great for the patch and the weakened boiler exploded.

The *Sultana* was also running on new experimental boilers. These new boilers had flues arranged in a zigzag fashion that made them very difficult to clean and increased the accumulation of sediment within the flue. This accumulation made the boilers susceptible to overheating or burning. While concluding that the repairs were the main cause of the explosion, Witzig agreed with Nathan Wintringer, chief engineer on the *Sultana*, that the accumulation of sediment in the flues put the *Sultana* at great risk.

Witzig put the blame for the disaster entirely upon the shoulders of Wintringer. He stated, "The boilers were imperfectly repaired at Vicksburg, which the engineer alone can be held responsible." He further stated, "When a boat leaves port, with machinery or engines in a bad condition, the law holds the engineer responsible." At the conclusion of his investigation, Witzig notified Nathan Wintringer that his engineer's license would be revoked. A short time later, the Board of Steamboat Inspectors in Washington issued its own order revoking Wintringer's license. Wintringer was furious and submitted a letter to the *Daily Missouri Democrat*, who published his denial of the charges and supposed facts.

He ended the letter by attacking Witzig saying, "I have been tried, condemned and executed without any hearing, by a man whose only qualification is to drink beer, and when he is on official duty is drunk half his time, and on his trip to Memphis fell into the river and came near drowning. I want only right and justice.

"I want the local Board of Inspectors to investigate my case, and on their decision I am willing to stand. What it may be, I do not know. I know they are practical men and know the law."

Two members of the board of inspectors under Witzig received his report and a copy of Wintringer's letter. After reviewing the documents and evidence, John Macquire and John Schaffer determined that either Nathan Wintringer, who survived the explosion, or Assistant Engineer Samuel Clemmons, who perished shortly after the incident, should be held responsible.

Aware that the dead could raise no defense, the inspectors found Clemmons to be the guilty party, completely ignoring their supervisor's report and the fact that Wintringer had approved the boiler repair. They refused to revoke Wintringer's license. They went on to say that Wintringer was in no way to blame for the incident since he was off-duty at the time of the explosion. [239]

Overcrowding of the *Sultana*

In the same inept way the investigation of the cause of
the *Sultana* explosion was handled, investigators in charge of
determining responsibility for the overcrowding were equally
incompetent. When the Confederates finally agreed to turn over
the prisoners to Union forces, Major General Napoleon Dana,
commander of the Department of Mississippi, ordered Captain
Frederick Speed to oversee the managing and loading of the
released prisoners from Camp Fisk to Vicksburg. [240]

At that time, two rival steamboat lines were vying for the
troops that were to be transported north. The *Henry Ames,* which
carried the first load of 1,300 released prisoners, was owned by the
Merchants and Peoples Line, while the second boat to leave, the
Olive Branch, was owned by the Atlantic and Mississippi Line and
carried 700 soldiers. The Merchants and Peoples Line had officially
contracted with the government to transport troops and freight,
but General Dana had instructed Captain Speed to place 1,000
soldiers on two of the non-contract steamers docked at Vicksburg.

During the process of loading the former prisoners onto those
two northbound steamers, rumors of bribery and kickbacks began
circulating. Because of these rumors, Captain Speed approached
General Dana and requested that he be allowed to arrest Captain
William Kerns, the assistant quartermaster in charge of river
transportation. Speed told Dana that Kerns had been ordered to

report arrival of all steamers to him.

He said that when the Olive Branch arrived at 1:00 a.m., Kerns had not informed him and that Kerns had received a "pecuniary consideration" by the Merchants and Peoples Line to hold the prisoners until one of its boats, which turned out to be the *Sultana*, arrived to take on the prisoners. General Dana said that he would not take any action against Kerns until a thorough investigation had taken place.

Speed had based his allegations against Kerns on information provided to him by Colonel Rueben Hatch, the chief quartermaster for the Department of Mississippi. As it turned out, Kerns had reported the arrival of the *Olive Branch* to Hatch, who was supposed to tell Speed. Apparently, Hatch failed to do this. Also, it was Hatch who had made the arrangements with the captain of the *Olive Branch* to transport prisoners. It is very likely that Hatch was the instigator and the recipient of any kickbacks from the Merchants and Peoples Line who then pointed the finger at Kerns in order to cover for his own misdeeds.

Captain J. Cass Mason of the *Sultana* had been promised a load of soldiers by Brigadier General Morgan L. Smith, commander of the post and the District of Vicksburg, when the *Sultana* was making its trip downriver. He also told Mason to let him know if Speed did not comply. [241]

When the *Sultana* returned to Vicksburg, the financially strapped Mason was on a mission to acquire as many troops as he could for his boat. He had first called on Colonel Hatch, who told him that Captain Speed had approximately 500 soldiers ready for release.

Mason said that would hardly be worth his staying until the next day, so Hatch suggested he check with Speed about obtaining a larger load.

Captain Speed did not want to send the next batch of troops on the *Sultana* and repeatedly stated that the rolls had not been sufficiently prepared to allow troops to be loaded on the boat. He shared this information with Captain Mason, who told Speed that his line, the Merchants and Peoples, still had an official contract with the government and should be given priority. [242]

Speed then upped the number to 700, but said that if Mason was willing to wait, he could have all the men that could be readied. Mason was not happy with Speed's response and headed for General Smith's office. When he arrived, he was introduced to Captain George Williams, the commissary of musters for the Department of Mississippi, who had just arrived at Vicksburg. Captain Mason made his feelings known about troops being shipped on another line when Merchants and People had a contract and said he was planning to register a complaint in Washington about the performance of the Mississippi Exchange Office.

Williams immediately assured Mason that he would have as many troops as he wanted, because the rolls could be prepared as the men were loaded and not in advance, as Speed had insisted.

Captain Speed was then summoned to the adjutant's office, where he, Williams, and Captain Mason discussed the situation with both sides arguing their cause.

Another meeting was then held with Williams, Speed, and Colonel Hatch. Speed insisted on preparing the rolls, and Williams maintained that the rolls could be prepared after the prisoners left by using the roll books provided by the Confederates.

Williams finally won the argument. It was then decided that all the prisoners at Vicksburg would be shipped on the *Sultana* on

April 24. The question then became whether or not it was the right thing to do and whether or not it was done because of fear over a complaint to Washington. At that moment, Captain Williams unknowingly sealed the fate of those who would lose their lives. [243]

Another fly in this ointment is that Captain Speed did not really know how many troops were left at Camp Fisk. There were far more than he believed. Although many voices were raised to question the mass of humanity on a ship built to hold 386 people, no action was ever taken to alter or resolve the situation.

So who was to blame? Obviously, there are many people who could have been brought up on charges, but only Captain Kerns, Colonel Hatch, and Captain Speed were indicted. Only Captain Speed was brought to trial. Though he was not entirely blameless, the man who had fought to the end to follow procedures and was overruled became the scapegoat. He was tried, convicted, court-martialed, and sentenced to dismissal from the service.

When the case was later reviewed by General Joseph Holt, the Judge Advocate General of the Army, he determined that, "Captain Speed took no such part in the transportation of the prisoners in question as should render him amendable to punishment," [244] thereby exonerating him and saving him from disgrace.

In the end, no one was held accountable for either the overloading or the explosion of the *Sultana*.

Andersonville Accountability

Despite an angry push to punish the Confederate leadership, because of problems experienced during the Lincoln assassination trial, President Andrew Johnson ordered that any charges against the Confederate generals and politicians should be dropped.

However, he did give his approval for Captain Henry J. Wirz, the commandant at Andersonville prison, to be charged with "wanton cruelty."

Indiana Major General Lew Wallace, who a little over two years after the Shiloh incident had been credited with saving Washington from a Rebel attack and had served on the military commission that oversaw the trial of the Lincoln conspirators, was chosen by President Johnson to head the military court to try Captain Wirz for his war crimes.

The conditions at Andersonville prison were inexcusable, irrespective of the many reasons given by Captain Wirz, but how cruel or compassionate Wirz was depends upon the source. During its 15 months of operation, the prison was widely regarded as hell on earth. After the war, several Andersonville inmates published their recollections of the experience, and some, but not all, portrayed Wirz as a cold-blooded monster.

Various accounts of Wirz's command at Andersonville describe contradictory aspects of his personality. Monster or not, he allowed the environment that caused such unbearable suffering and took so many precious lives. The prison had established a horrendous reputation in both the North and the South during its existence and upon closing a Federal investigation was ordered.

Following inspections of the site, the examination of prison records, and interviews with former prisoners, guards, and Wirz himself, the captain was arrested and put on trial.[245]

The charges filed against him included "Maliciously, willfully, and traitorously combining, confederating and conspiring to injure the health and destroy the lives of the prisoners of war so that the armies of the United States might be weakened and impaired; in violation of the laws and customs of war." A second charge was "Murder in violation of the laws and customs of war." It accused Wirz of deliberately murdering Union prisoners. The indictment accused him of causing death by, "Ordering a Sentinel to shoot a prisoner, shooting a prisoner with his revolver, jumping on and stamping a prisoner to death, beating a prisoner on the head with his revolver, having a prisoner attacked by vicious dogs, binding the necks and feet of prisoners with chains and iron balls and by confinement in the stocks."

Captain Henry Wirz

By modern legal standards the trial of Captain Wirz was filled with procedural errors and outright injustice. Wirz's defense presented credible evidence and testimony but the court allowed hearsay evidence to be admitted, ignored contradictory statements, and probably knew that much of the testimony was outright lies on the part of former prisoners who were justly angered by their harsh treatment.

In the end, to no one's surprise, Wirz was convicted on all but two charges and sentenced to hang. On November 3, 1865, just nine days after the trial ended, General Wallace read the guilty verdict and set the execution date as November 10, 1865. [246]

According to a Catholic priest who attended Wirz as he awaited execution, the captain was approached by unnamed government officials in the final days of his life and offered a deal that would save him from the gallows. Wirz was told that he would receive a presidential pardon if he would testify that Jefferson Davis ordered the atrocities at Andersonville. Wirz refused.

Seven days after his conviction, Captain Wirz was brought to the gallows amongst a mob scene that included 250 reporters and government officials who had received tickets for the event. Also present was a large frenzied crowd of drunk, angry, and curious spectators, including some Union troops.

Witnesses reported Major Russell, the officer in charge of the execution, apologized for the undignified way the execution was being carried out, saying he was only obeying his orders. Wirz replied, "I know what orders are, Major, and I am being hanged for obeying them." He then shouted, "I go before my God and almighty God who will judge between us. I am innocent, and I will die like a man."

A black hood was quickly placed over his head, the noose put in place, and the trap door sprung at exactly

Wirz hanging, with spectators in trees.

10:32 a.m. Unfortunately, the fall did not break his neck and he could be seen violently swinging and straining against the rope. The crowd went wild, yelling and cheering while the soldiers who came to view the hanging.

It has been debated whether or not the noose was improperly applied in order to cause Wirz as much embarrassment and pain as possible and intentionally causing the condemned man to slowly strangle to death.

Following the hanging, claims were made that his body languished unburied for three years. There were also rumors that Wirz's head had been removed and certain body parts sold.

Although none of the claims were substantiated, it is known that Wirz was originally buried in a grave beside George Atzerod, one of the Lincoln conspirators, on the grounds of the Washington Arsenal. He was later saved from that fate by his defense attorney Louis Schade. Schade purchased a headstone and a cemetery plot at the lone Catholic cemetery in the Washington, DC area. Only Schade and a Catholic priest attended the burial.

On the 125th anniversary of Wirz's death the Sons of Confederate Veterans and Colonel Heinrich Wirz, the great-grandnephew of the captain, organized and carried out a formal service in his honor.

An Episcopal priest presided over the ceremony and Confederate re-enactors used a three-inch mountain howitzer to fire a 21 gun salute and the grave was flanked by Confederate and Union flags.

No other person was charged or shared any responsibility for the conditions and deaths at the prison. [247]

9th Indiana Troops on Board the *Sultana*

Unit	Co.	Rank	Name	Fate
9th IN. Cav.	A	Sgt.	Curtis, Daniel	Died
9th IN. Cav.	A	Cpl.	Day, Elias R.	Lived
9th IN. Cav.	A	Pvt.	Day, Patrick	Died
9th IN. Cav.	A	Bugle	Evans, Charles	Lived, exhaustion
9th IN. Cav.	A	1st Sgt.	Hinckley, John B.	Lived, exhaustion
9th IN. Cav.	A	Pvt.	Paul, Arthur H.	Died May 6, 1865
9th IN. Cav.	A	Pvt.	Riley, William R.	Lived, bruised arm
9th IN. Cav.	A	Sgt.	Spades, Jacob	Lived
9th IN. Cav.	A	Sgt.	Tarkington, Robert	Lived, slight scalds
9th IN. Cav.	B	Cpl.	Blessinger, Frederick	Died
9th IN. Cav.	B	Pvt.	Church, Charles E.	Died
9th IN. Cav.	B	Pvt.	Gray, Joseph H.	Lived
9th IN. Cav.	B	Cpl.	Lyons, Virgil H.	Lived
9th IN. Cav.	B	Pvt.	Mooney, John	Lived
9th IN. Cav.	B	Pvt.	Parman, Ephriam B.	Died
9th IN. Cav.	B	Pvt.	Read, William P.	Lived
9th IN. Cav.	B	Pvt.	Scott, Robert S.	Lived
9th IN. Cav.	B	Pvt.	Sears, Christopher H.	Lived
9th IN. Cav.	B	Pvt.	Steward, John	Died
9th IN. Cav.	B	Pvt.	Waller, Benjamin F.	Lived
9th IN. Cav.	B	Pvt.	Warner, William C.	Lived
9th IN. Cav.	B	Pvt.	Wilson, George P.	Lived, chilled
9th IN. Cav.	C	Pvt.	Engelhart, John M.	Died May, 9, 1865
9th IN. Cav.	C	Pvt.	Huckins, Warren A.	Died
9th IN. Cav.	C	Pvt.	Kammer Thomas K.	Died
9th IN. Cav.	D	Pvt.	Wood, Edward	Died
9th IN. Cav.	E	Pvt.	Gilbreath, Robert W.	Lived, acute diarrhea
9th IN. Cav.	E	Pvt.	Laboyteaux, Thomas	Died June 7, 1865
9th IN. Cav.	E	Pvt.	McCormick, Andrew	Lived, uninjured
9th IN. Cav.	F	Pvt.	John Henry King	Lived, injured back
9th IN. Cav.	F	Pvt.	Pinion, Anderson	Lived, chilled
9th IN. Cav.	G	Cpl.	Allison, Hiram	Died
9th IN. Cav.	G	Pvt.	Clevenger, Charles W.	Died

9th IN. Cav.	G	Pvt.	Downing, George	Died
9th IN. Cav.	G	Pvt.	Downing, Jonathan R.	Died
9th IN. Cav.	G	Sgt.	Graves, William H.	Died
9th IN. Cav.	G	Pvt.	Hanna, Horton H.	Lived
9th IN. Cav.	G	Pvt.	Hoover, William C.	Died
9th IN. Cav.	G	Pvt.	Johnson, Lewis	Lived, bad burns
9th IN. Cav.	G	Pvt.	King, Charles William M.	Died
9th IN. Cav.	G	Pvt.	Kline, Henry J.	Lived neck, ear burns
9th IN. Cav.	G	Pvt.	Maynard, John M.	Died
9th IN. Cav.	G	Cpl.	Nation, Enoch K.	Died
9th IN. Cav.	G	Pvt.	Ollom, James C.	Died
9th IN. Cav.	G	Cpl.	Peacock, William H.	Lived scalds, cuts
9th IN. Cav.	G	Pvt.	Reasoner, John R.	Died
9th IN. Cav.	G	Sgt.	Rodepouch, Marvin V.	Died
9th IN. Cav.	G	1st Lt.	Swain, Elihue H.	Lived, exhaustion
9th IN. Cav.	G	Pvt.	Thornburg, Nathan	Died
9th IN. Cav.	H	Pvt.	Ballenger, Franklin	Died
9th IN. Cav.	H	Pvt.	Bell, James	Died
9th IN. Cav.	H	Pvt.	Delano, George W.	Died
9th IN. Cav.	H	Pvt.	Dunham, Alonzo	Died
9th IN. Cav.	H	Pvt.	Hardin, William H.	Lived
9th IN. Cav.	H	Pvt.	Mavity, Uriah J.	Lived
9th IN. Cav.	H	Pvt.	Pratt, Josiah	Died
9th IN. Cav.	H	Pvt.	Shull, John W.	Died
9th IN. Cav.	H	Pvt.	Stoops. Hermon B.	Lived
9th IN. Cav.	I	Pvt.	Hawthorn, Darius F.	Lived
9th IN. Cav.	K	Pvt.	Bailey, Hiram	Died
9th IN. Cav.	K	Pvt.	Baker, Oleo O.	Lived, uninjured
9th IN. Cav.	K	Pvt.	Block, William	Lived, slight contusion
9th IN. Cav.	K	Pvt.	Dorman, Henry	Died
9th IN. Cav.	K	Pvt.	Emmons, John W.	Died
9th IN. Cav.	K	Pvt.	Fisher, George S.	Died
9th IN. Cav.	K	Pvt.	Green, Seth J.	Lived, head, neck scalds
9th IN. Cav.	K	Pvt.	Harald, Jacob	Died
9th IN. Cav.	K	Pvt.	Kessler, Phillip	Lived, exhaustion
9th IN. Cav.	K	Pvt.	Laughlin. Thomas B.	Lived
9th IN. Cav.	K	Pvt.	Newton, Henry O.	Died
9th IN. Cav.	K	Pvt.	Rea, William F.	Died

9th IN. Cav.	K	Pvt.	Shockley, George H.	Died
9th IN. Cav.	K	Pvt.	Stevens, Darius	Died
9th IN. Cav.	K	Pvt.	Stokes, James	Lived
9th IN. Cav.	K	Pvt.	Survan, Joseph	Died
9th IN. Cav.	K	Pvt.	Windhorst, Jonathon	Lived
9th IN. Cav.	K	Pvt.	Zix, Matthew	Died
9th IN. Cav.	K	Pvt.	Survan, Joseph	Died
9th IN. Cav.	K	Pvt.	Windhorst, Jonathon	Lived
9th IN. Cav.	K	Pvt.	Zix, Matthew	Died
9th IN. Cav.	L	Sgt.	Addington, George W.	Lived
9th IN. Cav.	L	Pvt.	Christian, James R.	Died
9th IN. Cav.	L	Cpl.	Collins, William J.	Lived, uninjured
9th IN. Cav.	L	Pvt.	Daggy, George W.	Lived
9th IN. Cav.	L	Pvt.	Johnson, William T.	Lived
9th IN. Cav.	L	Pvt.	Johnston, James M.	Lived, chilled
9th IN. Cav.	L	Pvt.	Kelly, Grandison	Lived
9th IN. Cav.	L	Pvt.	McCartney, Leander	Died
9th IN. Cav.	L	Pvt.	Miller, Elias	Lived, slight scald
9th IN. Cav.	L	Pvt.	Moorhouse, Robert A.	Died
9th IN. Cav.	L	Pvt.	Reed, Archibald	Died
9th IN. Cav.	L	Pvt.	Winsor, William Henry	Lived. slight scald
9th IN. Cav.	M	Pvt.	Alexander, Joseph D.	Died
9th IN. Cav.	M	Cpl.	Armstrong, John M.	Died
9th IN. Cav.	M	Pvt.	Blake, George W.	Died
9th IN. Cav.	M	Pvt.	Brigg, John M.	Died
9th IN. Cav.	M	Cpl.	Brigg, William	Died
9th IN. Cav.	M	Pvt.	Chance, William H.	Died, severe scalds
9th IN. Cav.	M	Pvt.	Gaskill, David	Died
9th IN. Cav.	M	Cpl.	Gruell, Nathan	Died
9th IN. Cav.	M	Pvt.	Halloway, Enos	Died
9th IN. Cav.	M	Pvt.	Huffman, William H.	Died
9th IN. Cav.	M	Pvt.	Isentrager, William L.	Died
9th IN. Cav.	M	Pvt.	King, Samuel	Lived, uninjured
9th IN. Cav.	M	Pvt.	McGinnis, Samuel S.	Lived, uninjured
9th IN. Cav.	M	Pvt.	Ridley, Franklin	Died
9th IN. Cav.	M	Pvt.	Smith, Lorenzo	Lived
9th IN. Cav.	M	Pvt.	Spacey, Oscar F.	Lived
9th IN. Cav.	M	Farr	Watson Josiah	Lived, chilled

9th Indiana Cavalry Civil War Service

John King's unit, the 9th Indiana Cavalry, had been involved in action at Florence, Alabama on September 1 and 12; Elk River, Tennessee on September 2; Lynnville, Tennessee on September 4; Sulphur Branch Trestle, Tennessee on September 25; Richland Creek near Pulaski, Tennessee on September 26; and Pulaski, Tennessee on September 26-27. It served in the Nashville Campaign November and December and served post duty at Pulaski, Tennessee until November 23, 1864. It saw action at Owen's Cross Roads on December 1, Franklin on December 10, and the battle of Nashville December 15-16. It was in pursuit of Hood to the Tennessee River on December 17-28 and was at West Harpeth River and Hollow Tree Gap on December 17. It was in Franklin December 17, Lynnville December 23, Anthony's Hill near Pulaski December 25, and Sugar Creek December

9th Indiana Cavalry Battle Flag

25-26(where John King was captured). It was at Gravelly Springs, Alabama January 16 to February 6, 1865 and moved to Vicksburg, Mississippi, and thence to New Orleans, Louisiana, from February 6 to March 10. It returned to Vicksburg, Mississippi, and was on duty there March 25 to May 3. It went on expedition from Rodney to Port Gibson May 3-6 and served garrison duty at various points in Mississippi from May 3 to August 22. The Unit was mustered out on August 28, 1865.[248]

Dedication

*In memory of Cora May Smith (nee Adams), my paternal
grandmother and the granddaughter of John H. King*

I grew up in a home that included my mother, father, brother,
and two sisters, my father's brother, and my grandmother, Grandma
Smith. The eight of us, along with our dog Stubby, lived in a two-
bedroom bungalow on the east side of Indianapolis. My uncle
Raymond had one of the two bedrooms to himself, since he had
previously spent ten years at Sunnyside Sanitarium recovering from
tuberculosis, but was then in remission. This left one bedroom and
seven other people in the house. Mom, Dad, and my baby sister
Linda slept in that bedroom; my brother Dave slept in the dining

room on a daybed.
Grandma, my sister
Lois, and I slept in
the attic, which had
no heat in the winter
and no cool air in the
summer. Stubby the
dog slept under the
dining room table.

As I began to grow,
I started measuring my

Grandma and me

progress by standing next to Grandma.

Other than my baby sister, Grandma was the shortest one in the house. She was always willing to play along and remark on how close I was to catching up to her. One of my most special childhood memories with her is the day I stood face-to-face with Grandma and our noses touched.

~~~~~~

When I was about eight years old, my brother Dave was a teenager and already an accomplished magician. He gave performances at churches, clubs, parties, and various other events. I was his assistant, and I carried the "magic tricks" onto the stage during his act. I also had my own small part of the show: I continually emptied water from the same vase throughout the entire program. Grandma Smith thought I should dress properly for my role as magician's assistant, so she hand made a tuxedo for me from my cousin Bob's Coast Guard uniform. It was complete with shiny lapels and a stripe down the side of each pant leg. However, the wool material was so scratchy that I couldn't stand to wear the pants, but Grandma had a solution: I showed up at each performance wearing my pajama pants underneath my elegant tuxedo.

~~~~~~

After I had passed Grandma in height, I began to grow in other ways that were normal for young boys, namely growing some soft "peach fuzz" on my upper lip. One day I determined that the "fuzz" was too long and too dark and decided to shave it off. After lathering up and carefully using Dad's razor, I removed what I considered the offensive growth on my face. As I left the bathroom, the first person I encountered was Grandma. "Do you notice anything different?" I asked. She studied me for a long time, and then said, "No, I don't see anything." I said, "I shaved my moustache off!" Well, she laughed and laughed. I guess she laughed because she thought I was too young to shave or that I didn't need it. She then proceeded to take me by the arm and lead me through the house, looking for each family member and saying to them, "Look what Bobby did! He shaved off his moustache!" I felt a little embarrassed, but she was having so much fun that I didn't care.

~~~~~~

It was snowing lightly on December 13, 1964. As I was driving home from work, I decided that I would go see my grandmother at the nursing home that evening. By the time dinner was over, the snow had gotten quite heavy.

I began to wonder if I should make the trip. I had been told Grandma was very weak and had not responded to visitors recently. I decided to go anyway, because it had been awhile since I had seen her and I wanted to spend some time with her even if she couldn't respond. About halfway to the nursing home, the snow had gotten so deep that it was difficult to control the car.

I considered turning around and going home, but decided against it. I slipped and slid into the unplowed lot of the nursing home, chose a place away from the drifting snow, and parked. When I entered Grandma's room, I could see that her eyes were shut. She was partially covered by a sheet; one frail arm and leg were exposed. As I pulled the sheet to cover her up, she opened her eyes, looked at me, and said, "Bobby, I'm so glad you came." Her eyes shut again and she didn't speak another word while I was there. She died the next morning. R.R.S

Thanks to Crown Hill Cemetery John H. King received a

tombstone for his grave in May of 1993, one hundred years after his death.

Author and J.H. King Tombstone

Sultana Final Resting Place

As the flaming hulk of the *Sultana* approached an island in the river there were still several men riding on the bow of the ship. William Durkin, a deckhand, with severe burns on his face and hands, a gash on his face and his nose missing began yelling orders to several men to stop the *Sultana* from continuing downstream.

He told the men if they would grab the cable rope and tie it to some timber they could pull the boat up to the bank and secure it.

At that moment, Sgt. Michael J. Owens, Company I, 13th Indiana Cavalry was floating nearby holding on to a piece of siding. Beside him was Pvt. Riley Moore, Company D, 7th Kentucky Cavalry. The men on the bow tossed the end of the rope to the two men and instructed them to tie the rope to a line of trees on the bank.

Sgt. Owens made his way to a pile of island brush and tied the rope to a limb of a fallen tree. As the fire continued to rage, the section of unburned deck was growing smaller and the floor under the feet of the men was getting hot. But they kept on working, pulling on the rope and dragging the flaming wreckage toward the shore.

One of the men, Cpl. Wilson Fast, Company K, 102nd Ohio Infantry, later said, "Then we tied up the hull, and here she burned till she sank."

Since that time, the Mississippi river has rerouted itself and now lies approximately seven miles east of where the *Sultana* went down. The area, in Arkansas, is now a soybean field and the remnants of the *Sultana* are buried beneath twenty to thirty feet of earth. The high point of land on the right of the photo is believed to be the front edge of the island where the *Sultana* burned and sank in a cloud of steam.

Her final resting place beneath the plowed and fertile land
Under tons of dirt and sand
With no marker to tell the story
Of her time of tragedy or her days of glory.

More People Died in the *Sultana* Disaster than Did in the Sinking of the *Titanic*

The *Sultana* and the *Titanic* are extraordinary examples of similarities and contrasts. Most strikingly is the contrast in size. The *Titanic* measured 882.5 feet in length and 92.5 feet in width.

The *Sultana* was 260 feet long and 39 feet wide. The *Titanic* stood about 235 feet in height to the top of her smoke stacks making her taller than a twenty three-story building. The *Sultana* was 70 feet tall or about the height of a seven story building. However, despite the enormous difference in size, they amazingly were carrying nearly the same number of passengers. The *Titanic* carried 2,227 passengers and crew and the *Sultana*, with a few more, carried between 2,300 to 2,400 people.

Following the sinking of the *Titanic*, 705 people were rescued by Captain Arthur H. Rostron, skipper of the *Carpathia*, who had steamed 58 miles in four hours to facilitate the rescue.

With some last minute help from a private steamboat, the *Bostonia II*, the *Sultana* survivors initially numbered 783. However, approximately fifty

Titanic and *Sultana* comparison

one percent of those rescued died from scalds, burns, and injuries leaving just under 400 survivors.

The similarities between the *Sultana* and the *Titanic*, in addition to the number of passengers, include the month and times of both events. The *Sultana* disaster took place on April 27, 1865 when its boilers exploded at 2:00 a.m. just north of Memphis.

After striking the iceberg, the *Titanic* sunk to the bottom at 2:40 a.m. on April 15, 1912. Both events were triggered by the negligence of their Captains.

The *Titanic's* Catptain, Edward J. Smith, foolishly pushed the ship to its limit, racing at full speed across the Atlantic to break the speed record set by its sister ship the *Olympic*. Ignoring or disregarding warnings of ice flows and icebergs he sped ahead until it was far too late to avoid the collision. The ship was originally designed to carry 64 lifeboats on board but at the time of the crash there were only 16 available for the 2,227 passengers and crew resulting in the loss of more than 1,500 people.

Captain J. Cass Mason was equally negligent. The *Sultana* was built to carry 380 passengers and crew but he stood by and watched as over 2,000 troops were loaded on the ship in addition to the crew and passengers already on board. This was a ship that he had let fall into disrepair over the last year and at that very moment was having a leak in one of its boilers repaired.

Captain Mason also was negligent by allowing the ballast, (240,000 pounds of sugar) which counterbalanced the ship, to be removed and then did not replace it. Speed was also a factor in this tragedy as well. Mason's ship was trying to travel at normal speed despite the flood swollen river, the overloading of passengers and the poorly repaired boiler. A combination destined for disaster and the cause of over 1,800 deaths.

While the legend of the *Titanic* lingers on and continues to grow, the largest maritime tragedy in the history of the United States, the *Sultana* disaster, remains a lost chapter in the diary of our country.

End Notes

1. Godley's Ladies Book Magazine, Louis A. Godley, Publishers' Hall, Philadelphia, Thursday, April 9, 1840 Centennial History of Cincinnati, Charles Theodorc Greve, Biographical Publishing Company, Chicago, Ill. 1904 Page 793

2. 1829 - 30 & 1842 CINCINNATI CITY DIRECTORIES/1840 U.S. FEDERAL CENSUS

3. Excerpt: The Early Blacksmiths of Lancaster County, Elmer Z. Longenecker, Community Historians Annual, Number 10, Dec. 1971

4. Thomas Raymond Obituary Franklin County Democrat May 28, 1869, and Ancestry.com

5. Ancestry.com & The Church of Jesus Christ of Latter Day Saints http://www.family search.org Hester J. Raymond, Katherine

6. Hester J. Raymond-Ancestry.com and Men of Progress, Quintin Publications, 1991 Page 598

7. Men of Progress Publications 1991 Pages 596, 597- 1850-1860 U.S. Census Indiana and Indianans Author: Jacob Piatt Dunn Publshd. 1919, The American Historical Society, Vol. 5, Pg. 2268, Quintin

8. History of Decatur County, Indiana: its people, industries and institutions By Lewis Albert Harding. Pages 157, 158 Greensburg Gazeteer 1845. History of Indiana From its Exploration to 1922 Vol. IV By Logan Esarey. 1924

9. The Decatur Press October 1, 1852, 1850 U.S. Census.

10. Franklin County Indiana Marriage Records License issued October 5, 1849

11. Records of Decatur County Cemetery.

12. 1870 U.S. Census

13. Evolution of a Museum: A History of Conner Prairie http://www. connerprairie.org/Learn-And-Do/Indiana-History/Conner- Prairie-History/Conner-Prairie-History.aspx - October 2011. Indianapolis Monthly Oct 2003 Page 212/ History of Hamilton County, Indiana: her people, industries and Institutions. Volume 1 By John F. Haines Page 90

14. 1858 Indianapolis City Directory./http://www.butler.edu/about/ Wikipedia, the free encyclopedia. "Butler University". http:// en.wikipedia.org/wiki/Butler_University - cite_note-Butlerataglance-2

15. Decatur Republican Newspaper, February 12, 1856

16. Records of Decatur County Cemetery.
Pictorial and biographical memoirs of Indianapolis and Marion County By Goodspeed (Firm), publishers - Page 419

17. 1860 Census, http://www.shelbycountyindiana.org/historical_articles/ history_ch_lbr.htm

18. The New York Times New York May 23, 1860

19. King's not in Indiana or Ohio 1860 census, Nettie born in Cincinnati, 1861

20. Indianapolis Monthly, "The Van Camp Legend" April 1984, Page 100. and 1860 census.

21. 1870 Census Washington Township, Decatur County

22. The Successful American. January 1903 Page 674
Indiana Monthly, April 1984 Page 100
Decatur Republican Newspaper, March 6, 1857.
Decatur Republican Newspaper, September 15, 1856

23. Indianapolis Monthly, "The Van Camp Legend" April 1984

24. Decatur Republican Newspaper, September 15, 1856
March 6, 1857. Page 251 A Letter to Sarah, by Dorothy Robison.

25. Letter from Sarah: by Dorothy Robison

26. Indianapolis Monthly, "The Van Camp Legend" April 1984
    1860 Census. 1861 Bowen Stewart Indianapolis City Directory.

27. Indianapolis Monthly, "The Van Camp Legend" April 1984, Page 100,
    and 1860 census.

28. 1842 and 1860 Cincinnati City Directory.

29. Life Among the Soldiers and Cavalry by James A. Corrick
    Pages 7 and 8

30. Indiana and Indianans. Author: Jacob Piatt Dunn Published 1919,
    Pages 1562-1566

31. The Firing on Ft. Sumter a Splintered Nation Goes to War. Pages 15,
    16, 21, 26, 35, 36, 55, 78, 79, 94, 95. N.Y. Times. December 2, 1879

32. Biography of General Lew Wallace By Lew Wallace Harper & Brothers
    Publishers 1906 Pages 260 – 261

33. 1860 Census LOOKING BACK TO ARSENAL DAYS, by
    Ella Sengenberger

34. Greensburg Daily News, Greensburg, IN February 1861

35. Nettie's birth date September, 1861

36. Blue and Gray Civil War magazine. Volume XXI, Issue 4 Page 29
    Author Roger S. Durham. Indianapolis and the Civil War. Author: John
    Hampden Holliday Published by The Society of Indiana Pioneers with
    permissionof The Indiana historical Society 1972 Page 31.

37. Life Among the Soldiers and Cavalry by James A. Corrick Page 20

38. Crown Hill Cemetery, Find a Grave http://www.findagrave.com / Lost
    Indiana: In Grave Condition: Edward Black 1ST INDIANA HEAVY
    ARTILLERY REGIMENT RECORDS, 1861–1865

39. Nettie King birth record.

40. 1862 Indianapolis City Directory Page 225

41. Wallace/Grant at Shiloh; Shiloh and Corinth: sentinels of stone By Timothy T. Isbell - Page 23

42. George King birth record.

43. http://www.in.ng.mil/AboutUs/History/ HoosierCivilWarStoriesEliLilly/a bid/1489/Default.aspx July 17, 2012 Major H. Allen Skinner TF East OIC http://www.usgwarchives.net/pensions/civilwar/inindex6.htm 7/20/2012 Indiana Recruiting and Retention Battalion Indiana National Guard http://www.paralumun.com/lilly.htm July 18, 2012 Eli Lilly and Company Archives Archival information provided by Lilly Corporation through Ms. Lisa Bayne, Lilly Corporation historian. Eli Lilly Historical Marker, Greenfield, Indiana.

44. Brief History of Lilly's Battery, 18th Indiana Light Artillery, Copyright 2003 Page 1

45. Transport to Disaster Author: James W. Elliot Publisher, Holt Rinehart and Winston Copyright 1962 Pages 14,15

46. Disaster on the Mississippi, Gene Salecker Pages 7 thru 12

47. The Life of General John Hunt Morgan by James A. Ramage Page 89 Active Service - Author John B. Castleman Page 189 - 1860 Census

48. Crown Hill Cemetery, Find a Grave http://www.findagrave.com / Lost Indiana: In Grave Condition: Edward Black 1ST INDIANA HEAVY ARTILLERY REGIMENT RECORDS, 1861–1865 The Story of Crown Hill. Author Anna Nicholas Published 1928. Page 41 The Indianapolis Star June 4, 1924,Indianapolis Daily Journal May 30, June 1, June 2, 1864. Crown Hill Burial Locator, 1860. The Seaton family, with genealogy and biographies. Page 358. By Oren Andrew Seaton. Publisher: Topeka, Kansas, Crane and Company 1906. Louisville Journal, January 21, 1860. 1893. Ancecstry.com U.S. Civil War Soldiers 1861–1865.Letter from attorney for son John H. Seaton December 16, 1933. Harrison County Kentucky marriage records 1794–1893. Find A Grave Memorial, http://www.findagrave.com/cgi-

bin/fg.cgi?page=gr&GSln= Seaton&GS. Family Search.org Tennessee Marriages 1796-1950. Ancestry.com Hart Family Tree, owner Leon Hart.1850,1860 and 1880 U.S. Census.

49. Disaster on the Mississippi, Gene Salecker Pages 7, 9.

50. Lee's Real Plan at Gettysburg : By Troy D. Harman Pages 9, 10

51. The Battle of Gettysburg: a guided tour By Edward James Stackpole, Wilbur Sturtevant Nye, Bradley M. Gottfried. Pages 47,48, 49 Publisher; Stackpole Books

52. Gettysburg: Sentinels of Stone By Timothy T. Isbell Page 96

53. The Battle of Gettysburg and Lincoln's Gettysburg Address. Enslow Publishers Inc. Author Carin T. Ford Pages 6 through 36, Legion of Valor, homeofheroes.com

54. "What they did here": Historical guide book By Luther William Minnigh page 138, http://www.gettysburg. stonesentinels.com/IN.php

55. The Morgan Raid in Indiana and Ohio" Author: Arville F. Funk Copyright 1971 by Author. Page 4

56. Days of Glory: The Army of the Cumberland. Pages 227, 232

57. When Johnny Went Marching: Young Americans Fight the Civil War. Clifton Wisler Page 75 Hazzard's history of Henry county, Indiana, 1822-1906, Volume 1 By George Hazzard Page 234 Days of Glory: The Army of the Cumberland Pages 298, 299 Author: Larry J. Daniel U.S. National Park Service U.S. Library of Congress.http:// americancivilwar.com/statepic/tn/tn018.html http://www.nps.gov/archive/chch/hrs/history.htm http://historynet.com/battle-of-chicamauga-colonel-john-t-wilder-and-the-lightening-brigade.htm & Eli Lilly A Life/Indiana's War; The Civil War Documents.

58. The Battle of Gettysburg and Lincoln's Gettysburg Address. Enslow Publishers Inc. Author Carin T. Ford Pages 33 through 39

59. G.S.A. Military Records John H. King
121st Regiment, 9th Indiana Cavalry, Company F Adjutant Generals Report Company Descriptive Book

60. Hoosiers in the Civil War Author: Arville F. Funk Nugget Publishers Copyright 1967

61. Indiana Guardsman: A Look Back at the Civil War: Eli Lilly Major H. Allen Skinner Indiana Recruiting and Retention Battalion Indiana National Guard Railroad Wars Pages 70,

62. Camp Morton Authors; Mattie Lou Winslow & Joseph R. M. Moore Published 1940 by Indiana Historical Society Press Pages 3,4 and 6. A Historical and Statistical Sketch of the Railroad City. Author; W.R. Holloway Indianapolis Journal print-1870 Ch.113 Page 118

63. Cooke's Cavalry Tactics Manual

64. Buford's Boys by J. David Petruzzi Copyright 2000 – 2005

65. Disaster on the Mississippi Author Gene Salecker Page 9.

66. Indiana Battle Flag Commission. Battle Flags and Organizations Page 625

67. Daily Evening Gazette, Indianapolis May 3, 1864 Page 1.

68. Daily Evening Gazette, Indianapolis May 3, 1864 City Section

69. William V. Wheeler Diary, May 4, 6, 1864

70. Civil War Indiana, Indiana Regimental Histories.
William V. Wheeler Letter, May 24, 1864
Civil War Regiments from Indiana, 1861-1865

71. William V. Wheeler Diary, May 25, 26, 1864

72. Memorial Address on the life and character of John Franklin Miller Washington Government Printing Office, 1887

73. William V. Wheeler Diary, May 23, 1864

74. William Wheeler Diary – May 27, 28.

75. The 1864 Capture of Eli Lilly, Author, Richard Young, Page 1

76. Indiana's General's report. War of the Rebellion, Civil War Unit History. Regimental Histories E-464-U6-1985 Series n1 Part 1, Vol.45 Page 606.

77. William Wheeler Diary – June 8, 10, 1864

78. The Artillery of Nathan Bedford Forest's Cavalry. Author: John Watson Morton Publishing House of the M.E. Church. Chapter 18, Page 233

79. 9th Indiana Cavalry Author Daniel Webster Comstock. Publisher J.M. Coe, Richmond, Indiana, 1890. Page 9

80. 9th Indiana Cavalry Author Daniel Webster Comstock. Publisher J.M. Coe, Richmond, Indiana, 1890. Page 3

81. Corporal J.A. Brown report. U.S. Military History Research Collection. Civil War Unit Histories. Part 4 Indiana. Page 16.

82. 9th Indiana Cavalry Author Daniel Webster Comstock. Publisher J.M. Coe, Richmond, Indiana, 1890. Pages 2, 3, 4.

83. The Railroad War.71, 72, 140. "History of Pottawattamie County Iowa PUBL. O.L. Baskin & Company Chicago 1883, Page 244.

84. End Note: William Wheeler Diary, Nov. 25, 1864 http//gunsandammo. com/content/maynards-masterpiece Pages 28, 29.

86. William Wheeler Diary November 27, 28.1864

87. Ninth Indiana Cavalry Daniel Webster Comstock P. 26 Diary William V. Wheeler Diary, Nov. 30, 1864

88. Nashville: the Western Confederacy's Final Gamble By James L. McDonough, Pages 72,73. From Ashville to Tuscumbia A Brief Account of Hood's Retreat By David Fraley and O.C. Hood

89. Every day of the Civil War: a chronological encyclopedia By Bud
    Hannings Page 494.
    From Nashville to Tuscumbia A Brief Account of Hood's Retreat
    By David Fraley and O.C. Hood
    Ninth Indiana Cavalry, 121st Regiment, Indiana Volunteers. Published
    by J.M. Coe, Richmond, Indiana –1890. Pages 27 – 31. Diary - William
    V. Wheeler, November 30. December 1, 1864.
    The National Park Service. Department of the Interior, Category:
    Indiana - Military - Civil War, 1861-1865, Report of the Adjutant
    General of the State of Indiana, Volume 3, 1860 Census

90. Casualties from the 1864 Tennessee Campaign Retreat,
    December 17–26, 1864, The Carter House, Franklin, TN.
    Every day of the Civil War: a chronological encyclopedia
    By Bud Hannings Page 494
    Descendants of John Randall http://crandallgenealogy.com/
    robertcrandall.html.
    Wyatt Crandall, Company E, 9th Indiana Cavalry. Killed at Franklin,
    Tennessee, December 17. 1864. Buried on the battlefield. Re-interred
    In Nashville National Cemetery. Unknown list.

91. Curtis Hancock Letter, Indiana Historical Society Collection.

92. US Army Quartermaster Foundation Fort Lee, Virginia, FEEDING
    BILLY YANK: Union Rations between 1861 and 1865 By J. Britt
    McCarley Quartermaster Professional Bulletin – December 1988
    Civil War Diary of William Wheeler 9th Indiana Cavalry, Company D
    December 1864.

93. "Tennessee Confederate Prisoners at Camp Morton" Author: Don
    Allen Augustus Lillard letter – June 27, 1864.
    The Healing Power of Water By Masaru Emoto Publisher Hay House
    Inc. 2004 Page 22 civilwaracademy.com/civilwar-html   "Food"
    Oct. 13, 2012 http://www.civilwar.org/education/pdfs/civil-war-
    curriculum-food.pdf   Oct. 13, 2012

94. Ninth Cavalry, Daniel Webster Comstock Page 26

95. Diary of the 4th Regiment Tennessee Cavalry, Volunteers - by James
    W. Godwin Co. E. 4th Reg. Tenn. Cavalry, Volunteers. Louisianians in

the Western Confederacy: Stuart Salling, McFarland & CO. Inc. Page 217 William Wheeler Diary Dec. 1 – 16

96. 1870 Census
9th Cavalry, 121st Regiment Indiana Volunteers. Publ. By J.M. Coe 1899, Page 26

97. The Civil War Memoirs of Phillip Daingerfield,D.D.Page 340

98. Indiana Generals Report War of the Rebellion Civil War Unit Histories, Regimental Histories E 464-U6-1985 Series 1 Pat 1 Vol. 45 Pages 606, 607. J.H. King Military brecords Affidavit John H. Thompson. Franklin and Beyond   by Benjamin Franklin Cooling Page. 334. William Wheeler Diary Dec.25, 1864. John H. King Military Records Single Affidavit,

99. Single Affidavit of John W. Thompson Notarized June 9, 1890. 1860 U.S. Census ohn W. Thompson, June 9, 1890

100. William Wheeler Diary, December 24, 25, 1864 To the Battles of Franklin and Beyond by Benjamin Franklin Cooling Page. 334

101. U.S.A. Pension Records, John H. King 121st Regiment, 9th Indiana Cavalry, Company F. 1860 U.S. Census.
Life of General Nathan Bedford Forrest
By John Allan Wyeth Pages 560 through 572
The Death of An Army: The Battle of Nashville and Hood's Retreat. Publisher, Southern Heritage Press 1992. Author; Paul H. Stockdale Page 156
George H. Thomas, Major General U.S.A. "The Rock of Chickamauga," "The Sledge of Nashville."

102. Soldiers Blue and Gray Author James I. Robertson Publisher University of South Carolina Press, 1988 Page 143

103. Indiana Generals Report, War of the rebellion Civil War Unit History Regimental histories. E-464-U6-1985 Series 1, Part 1, Volume 45 Page 608

104. Soldiers Blue and Gray Author James I. Robertson Publisher University of South Carolina Press, 1988 Page 143

105. Daily Evening Gazette, December 24, 1864, Wm. Seymour Theatre Collection Princeton University, "The Players" Jan. 2, 1860. The Encyclopedia of Indianapolis By David J. Bodenhamer, Robert Graham Barrows Page 149

106. Indiana Generals Report, War of the rebellion Civil War Unit History Regimental histories. E-464-U6-1985 Series 1, Part 1, Volume 45 Page 772, March 7, 1883

107. U.S. Military Records, John H. King, Affidavit: Anderson Pinion

108. Nashville to Tuscumbia: A Brief Account of Hood's Retreat. David Fraley and O.C. Hood

109. Descendants of John Crandall http://candallgenealogy.com/civilwar. html. #'s 11 and 103 October, 2011

110. Casualties from the Tennessee Campaign Retreat December 17 thru 26, 1864 John B. Hood Historical Society Page 6

111. History of Andersonville Prison Author Ovid L.Futch 1968 Pages 2,3

112. History of Andersonville Prison Author Ovid L.Futch 1968 Page 5

113. History of Andersonville Prison Author Ovid L.Futch 1968 Page 10

114. Life and Death in Civil War Prisons J. Michael Martinez, Rutledge Hill Press Pages 771, 774

115. Andersonville Journey Edward F. Roberts, Burd Street Press Page 28

116. The True Story of Andersonville Prison. Authors; James Madison Page, Michael Jochim Haley. Page 78. The Neale Publishing Company 1908

117. History of Andersonville Author, Ovid L. Futch Copyright 1966, Page 107.

118. Loss of the Sultana and reminiscences of Survivors. Author, Rev. Chester D. Berry Pages 338, 339

119. Sultana Newsletter, Fall 2005/Winter 2006

120. Sultana Newsletter, Fall 2005/Winter 2006

121. 12 Months in Andersonville. Publisher Huntington, Ind., T. and M. Butler Published 1886

122. Blue and Gray Chaplain Fr. Peter Whelan: Serving the Blue and the Gray Part 2: Andersonville Author Ed Churchill

123. Portals to Hell Author, Lonnie R. Speer Published 1977 Page 577

124. Andersonville Journey, Burd Street Press 1998 Author Edward F. Roberts Pages 40 – 53.

125. John H. King Military Records, March 7, 1883

126. John H. King General Affidavit of James H. Kimberlin, Andesonville Medical ecos.

127. http://civilwar.bluegrass.net/CasualtiesAndMedicalCare/ medications.html

128. GSA Pension Records, John H. King, Adjutant Generals Office War Dept. March 7, 1883.
History of Andersonville Prison Author Ovid . L. Futch University of Florida Press Book 1968 Page 107

129. Andersonville Prison Records, Indiana Soldier Deaths. Notes from Charles Terhune Duncan

130. http://web.usi.edu/boneyard/mccutc66.htm 9/2/2011

131. A Melancholy Affair at the Weldon Railroad JUNE 23,1864/Narrative Accounts/The Deadly Hookworm/David F. Cross, MD.

132. History of Andersonville Author, Ovid L. Futch Copyright 1968, Page 109

133. History of Andersonville Author, Ovid L. Futch Copyright 1968, Page 106

134. Quick Step News. Civil War Roundtable of Montgomery County PA. February 2004, Page 2.

135. The Sultana Tragedy Author; Jerry O.Potter Pelican Publishing 1992 Page 43, Disaster on the Mississippi, Author: Gene Salecker. Publisher, Naval Institute Press page 11

136. Civil War and Reconstruction (1850-1877) By Jody Cosson Page 19. Weigl Publishers Inc. 2008 Gideon Luke Roach "Confederate Veteran", vol. 34, page 73 The Hannah Page, wife of Gideon Luke Page, aklinger@charter.net Ancestry.com.

137. Kim Douglas, Lead Park Ranger Andersonville National Historic Site, Andersonville Georgia.

138. Report on Gangrene A. Thornburgh, Assistant Surgeon, ,Provisional Army, C.S. From January 1, 1865

139. Andersonville Prison Records, Indiana Soldier Deaths.Notes: Gary Sacre, Great, Great nephew of George O. Huston. 1860 Federal Census

140. History of Andersonville. Front inside book jacket. The Tragic Story of Tom Horan by Kenneth P. McCutchan The Evansville, Boneyard March 2007. 141. The Tragic Story of Tom Horan by Kenneth P. McCutchan. The Evansville Boneyard - March, 2007

142. Genealogy Trails History Group. The Sultana Disaster by Joseph Taylor Elliot. Genealogy Story Group 1913, Page 1 http:// genealogytrails.com/main/events/sultanadisaster.html 2014

143. Indiana and the Indianians Author Jacob Piatt Dunn. The American Historical Genealogy Trails History Group. The Sultana Disaster by Joseph Taylor 1913, Pages 1,2,3. Loss of the Sultana and Remembrances of Survivors. Chester Berry Pages 304, 305. Alonzo Githers general affidavit April 9, 1883.

144. Sultana-D Digest V99 #61 August 3, 1999 by Gene Salecker Page 2

145. Report of the Adjutant General War of the Rebellion 1861 – 1865 Officers Regiments 75 – 156 and other service. 1866 Page 231

146. G.S.A. Pension Records John H. King. General Affidavit filed with Clerk of the Circuit Court Marion County Indiana
Filed May 14, 1883.
Military records John H. King. General Affidavit of Alonzo Githers April 9, 1883. Military Records John H. King Certificate Of Disability Capt. N.J. Owings, April 12, 1883.

147. The Sultana Disaster by Joseph Taylor Elliot. Genealogy Story Group 1913, Page 3

148. Transport to Disaster, James W. Eliott Copyright 1962 Page 43.
Loss of the Sultana and Remembrances of Survivors, Chester D. Berry
Page 39.

149. Transport to Disaster James W. Elliot Page 46
Transport to Disaster Author: James W. Elliot Copyright 1962 Pages 16, 17, 34

150. Disaster on the Mississippi, Gene Salecker Pages 29, 30, 31.

151. Civil War Times Illustrated, Author Frank R. Lvstik
January 1967 Page 20

152. The Sultana Tragedy Author Jerry Potter Page 162
Transport to Disaster, James W. Elliot 1962 Pages 53, 54.

153. J.H. King Individual Muster Out Roll August 4, 1865
Transport to Disaster, James W. Elliot Copyright 1962 Pages 62, 63,59

154. Transport to Disaster, James W. Elliot Copyright 1962 Pages 62,63
The Sultana Tragedy Author; Jerry O. Potter 1992 Page 70

155. Tennessee History Quarterly Wilson M. Yeager. Fall 1976 Page 312

156. Disaster on the Mississippi, Gene Salecker Page 51,58
Indiana History Bulletin Vol's 31, 32 Robert Talkington

157. John H. King Pension Records. John H. Thompson May 19,1888
Transport To Disaster Author James W. Elliot
Copyright 1962 Pages 81, 82

158. Disaster on the Mississippi, Gene Salecker Page 67
Tennessee History Quarterly Wilson Yeager. Fall of 1976 Pg. 313

159. Disaster on the Mississippi, Gene Salecker Page 72
Hancock County Indiana Civil War Soldiers Plus related Facts. P. 475

160. Transport to Disaster, James W. Elliot Copyright 1962 Pages 86, 87

161. Disaster on the Mississippi, Gene Salecker Page 75
Transport to Disaster, James W. Elliot Copyright 1962 Page 88
Sultana Remembered Newsletter-Fall 2005/Winter 2006 Page 2.

162. Tennessee History Quarterly, Fall of 1976 Page 314
Disaster on the Mississippi, Gene Salecker Pages 77, 230
Loss of the Sultana and Reminiscences of Survivors
Chester D. Berry Page 126

163. Transport to Disaster, James W. Elliot Copyright 1962
Pages 82, 99, 100

164. Loss of the Sultana and Remembrances of Survivors,
Chester D. Berry Pages 301, 63, 64.

165. Loss of the Sultana and Remembrances of Survivors,
Chester D. Berry Pages 116, 117, 118

166. Sultana Remembered Newsletter Fall 2005/Winter 2006 Pages 2, 3.
Disaster on the Mississippi, Gene Salecker Page 100.

167. Loss of the Sultana and Remembrances of Survivors,
Chester D. Berry Page 377, 378.

168. Loss of the Sultana and Reminiscences of Survivors
C.D. Berry Pages 185, 186

169. Transport to Disaster James W. Elliot Copyright 1962
Pages 124, 125
Indiana History Bulletin, Vol's. 31, 32. Robert Talkington
Sultana and Disaster on the Mississippi, Gene Salecker Page 78
Loss of the Sultana and Reminiscences of Survivors C.D. Berry
Pages 285, 286, Hazard's History of Indiana. 1822-1906 Volume 1
Pages 612 – 617

170. The Union Standard Dec. 2005 Vol. 13 #9

171. The Wellington (Kansas) Daily News May, 25, 1933
The Washington Times- June 25, 2008

172. American Heritage Magazine. "Death on the Dark River, October 1955
Page 4. Transport to Disaster, James W. Elliot 1962 Page 131.
Death on the Mississippi, Salecker, Page 115

173. Loss of the Sultana and Reminiscences of Survivors C.D. Berry
Pages 320, 321.

174. Loss of the Sultana and Reminiscences of Survivors C.D. Berry
Pages 249, 250, 32.

175. Tennessee History Quarterly. Author, Wilson M. Yeager
Fall 1976 Page 315

176. I Loss of the Sultana and Reminiscences of Survivors
Author. Rev. Chester D. Berry Page 381.
Indianapolis Evening Gazette May 3, 1865 Page 2

177. Loss of the Sultana and Reminiscences of Survivors C.D. Berry
Page 209

178. 9th Indiana Cavalry, 121st Regiment Indiana Volunteers
Published 1890, J.M. Coe Richmond, Indiana Page 54.

179. The Sultana Tragedy Author; Jerry O.Potter Pelican Publishing 1992
Page 131. 9th Indiana Cavalry, 121st Regiment Indiana Volunteers
Published 1890, J.M. Coe Richmond, Indiana Page 51.

180. John H. King Pension records Single affidavit April, 20, 1888
John H. King Proof of Disability affidavit Anderson Pinion
May 17, 1890.

181. Daily New York Tribune Saturday May 13, 1865

182. Tennessee History Quarterly Wilson M. Yeager Fall 1976 Page 319

183. Fayette County Kentucky Genealogoical Pamphlet Winter 1990 Page 101

184. Transport To Disaster James W. Elliot 192, Pages 224, 225.

185. The Indianapolis Daily Evening Gazette, April 29, 1865 Page 3

186. The Daily Indiana Sentinel, May 2, 1865 page 3.

187. The Indianapolis Daily Journal, April 29, 1865 Page 1

188. Sultana Monument in Mt. Olive Cemetery, Knoxville, TN.

189. Disaster on the Mississippi Gene Salecker, Page 210

190. GSA Pension Records John H. King Single Affidavit April 20, 1888.

191. Disaster on the Mississippi Gene Salecker, Page 181.

192. Loss of the Sultana and Reminiscences of Survivors C.D. Berry
     Pages 21, 252 209

193. Disaster on the Mississippi Gene Salecker, Pages 183, 184.

194. Indianapolis Daily Journal, May 1, 1865 Page 1 & The Lincoln
     Funeral Train Memorial Plaque, Indianapolis.

195. Newsletter of the Association of Sultana Descendants Author:
     Gene Eric Salecker Vol. 5 No.12 Winter 1995 Page 2.
     Disaster on the Mississippi Author: Gene Salecker pgs. 183, 184

196. The last Battle of the Civil War. Author: Jeffery Wm. Hunt University
     of Texas Press 2002.

197. Report of the Chief of Engineers U.S. Army by United States Army
     Corps of Engineers. Page 1444, The Vicksburg Daily Journal
     August 22, 1866 Colonel Lilly Biography
     Lilly Archives Pages 4, 5.

198. Time line and growth of Van Camp business.

199. Military Discharge Records August 28, 1865, Family Photographs.

200. http://www.findagrave.com - Lost Indiana: In Grave Condition
     www.lostindiana.net/html/crown_hill__black.html Edward Black
     1ST Indiana heavy Artillery Regiment records, 1861-1865.

201. 1867 Indianapolis city directory.

202. 1870 U.S. Census.

203. American Law Record: Vol. II Superior Court of Cincinnati, General Term, May, 1873. SARAH VAN CAMP v. ALDRICH & COMPANY. Franklin Democrat Newspaper, August 11, 1870.

204. 1875 Indpls. City Directory.

205. Ancestry/History Orb.com, History in the 1870's. Lippincott's New Gazetteer: Geographical Dictionary J.B. Lippencott Company Page 873. The History of the Studebaker Company Author: Albert Erskine Published 1918. Page 29

206. John H. King pension records. Single Affidavit Oct. 10. 1889. Indianapolis News April 24, 1892 Page 12.

207. Greater Indianapolis: the history, the industries, the ..., Vol.1 By Jacob Piatt Dunn The 1880 census, The Indianapolis Daily Sentinel Jan. 18, 1879

208. 1880 Indianapolis City Directory

209. A Letter To Sarah Author Dorothy Robison January, 1987.

210. John H. King Pension Records Single Affidavit August 1, 1882 Polk's Indianapolis 1878 City Directory Page 321 Polk's Indianapolis 1879 City Directory Page 297

211. The State Military Pension System of Tennessee William H. Glasson Sage Publications Inc. Page 95. "Encyclopedia of the American Civil War" edited by David S. Heidler and Jeanne T. Heidler, page 1489.

212. John H. King Pension Records, single affidavit of John H. Thompson June 9, 1890.

213. J.H. King Pension files. Letter from H. Fisher, Nov.25, 1889. 1900 U.S. Census. John H. King military records. Examining Surgeons certificate, Dr. Henry Jameson September 27, 1882. John H. King Military Records, Increase Invalid Pension, New Disability Reject December 10, 1886.

214. Oswego Palladium October 5, 1891. Page 3.

215. Entrepreneur magazine encyclopedia of entrepreneurs By Anthony Hallett, Diane Hallett Page 463,   LIFE MAGAZINE MARCH 10, 1941, History of Indiana From Its Exploration to 1922 With an Account of Indianapolis and Marion County Vol. IV by Logan Esarey. Dayton Historical Publishing Co1924, 1870, 1880 and 1900 Census Oswego Palladium October 5, 1891. Page 3, A History of the canning Industry Author: Arthr Ignatius Judge Page 19, Printers ink Volumes 64-65 Vol. XLV, New York, October 14, 1908 No.3 Page 4.

216. John H. King Military Records, Original Invalid Pension Sept.6, 1883

217. John H. King Military Records, General Affidavits May 5, 14, 28, April 3, 1883 Invalid Certificate #250696 Sept. 23, 1892.
John H. King Military Records, Increase Invalid Pension
New Disability Reject Filed December 10, 1886.

218. Notarized request for Pension Increase December 1, 1886
Prepared by W.H. Corbaly. Witnessed by Oliver Rice and Michael Nye.

219. G.S.A. Pension Records Declaration for Increase John H. King
Notarized December 19, 1887.

220. John H. King Military Records, Surgeons Certificate, Danville, Indiana April 20, 1887

221. John H. King Military Records Single Affiavit
Notarized June 11, 1887

222. Indianapolis-Marion County Register of Historic Properties, Nomination Form, prepared by the Indianapolis Historic Preservation
Commission, June 27, 1983. Ernestine Bradford Rose, The Circle: The Center of Indianapolis, Indianapolis: Crippin Printing Corporation, 1971.

223. John H. King U.S. Government Pension Records
Invalid Certificate #250696 September 23, 1892
Military Records John H. King
Surgeons Report, Indianapolis, Indiana

224. The New York Times, March 14, 1901, Page 1

225. John H. King Military Records Single Affidavit Michael W. Nye October 8, 1889. General Affidavit Seth Green May 21, 1883 Letter from Seth Green November 27, 1889. 1890 Census, 1891 Indianapolis City Directory, Medical Evidence Document. John H. King. Pension Files Sept. 1891.

226. H.Fisher letter from J.H. King pension files, 1900 U.S. Census.

227. Family oral history. J.H. King Pension Records Single Affidavit Notarized October 10, 1889. J.H. King Military Records, letter of Dr. C.E. Crose October 7, 1889.

228. Indianapolis Journal, May 24, 1902 Page4

229. Letter from W.L. Bartlett Ambia, Indiana to Samuel Sawyer Indianapolis, Indiana March 17, 1893.

230. John H. King Military Records Surgeons Certificate Noblesville, Indiana Sepember 3, 1890. Invalid Pension Form 3-145 Thomas D. Ingram Medical Referee, June 20, 1892

231. Indianapolis City Directory 1889 Indiana and Indianians Author Jacob Piatt Dunn Page 2269

232. Kurt Vonnegut Memorial Library. Vonnegut Family History – Clemmons Vonneegut by Rebeccah February 17, 2010.

233. John H. King Military Records Surgeons Certificate, Indianapolis, Indiana November 5, 1891.

234. John H. King letter to granddaughter Cora May Adams Nov. 11, 1892

235. Discharge Form #31 Certificate 250696 Hoboable Commssioner of Pensions Washington D.C. National Home for D.V.S. Marion, Indiana Form #25 H.A. Sainchart Treasuruer. John H. King Death Certificate. Crown Hill Cemetery Grave Registration Form #1. The American Legion.

236. Indianapolis Sentinal Page 7, May 24, 1893. Crown Hill Burial Locator.

Crown Hill Burial Locator and
Katherine King tombstone.

237. Original Diary of Raymond James Smith 1933–1935.

238. Loss of the Sultana and Reminiscences of Survivors C.D. Berry
Pages 12, 13

239. The Sultana Tragedy Author; Jerry O.Potter Pelican Publishing 1992
Pages 153, 154, 155, 156, 157.

240. The Sultana Tragedy Author; Jerry O.Potter Pelican Publishing 1992
Page 49

241. The Sultana Tragedy Author; Jerry O.Potter Pelican Publishing 1992
Pages 50, 51, 47

242. Disaster on the Mississippi, Gene Salecker Pages 40, 41.

243. The Sultana Tragedy Author; Jerry O.Potter Pelican Publishing 1992
Page 53.

244. Disaster on the Mississippi, Author Gene Salecker
Naval Institute Press 1996 Pages 42, 43, 200.

245. Andersonville Journey, Author, Edward F. Roberts Page 96.
http://www.Spartacus.schoolnet.co.uk/USACWwirz.htm Page

246. Andersonville Journey, Author, Edward F. Roberts Pages 112,
113, 142, 143, 145, 146, 147, 148, 149. The Sword and the Pen,
A Life of Lew Wallace 1959, Ray Boomhower Pages 85, 86.
Ask.Com http://www.spartacus.schoolnet.co.uk/USACWwirz.htm.
Page 2

247. Andersonville Journey, Author, Edward F. Roberts Pages 112, 113,
142, 143, 145, 146, 147, 148, 149.

248. "The Union Army" by Federal Publishing Company, 1908
Volume 3, Page 179.

249. Disaster on the Mississippi, Author Gene Salecker
Naval Institute Press 1996 Pages 226 through 239.

About the Author

Robert R. Smith retired after 45 years in Indiana broadcasting. He began as a film editor/ photographer, then producer/director then Production Manager at WISH TV.

During his time at WISH TV Bob produced and directed several nationally syndicated programs. He later became Program Manager and Station Manager for WIPB TV Ball State University. He retired from Ball State in 2001.

He is a Board Member of the Indiana Broadcast Pioneers and writes and produces the organization's quarterly newsletter.

The inherited "before and after" photos in the book and his interest in genealogy led to the search for more information which became the foundation for this book.

Bob attended Arsenal Technical High School and Indiana Central College and served in the Indiana National Guard for six years as a motion picture photographer with training at Fort Leonard Wood Missouri and Fort Monmouth, New Jersey.

Bob is married to high school sweetheart Bette. He has two children, Darren and Lori, and five grandchildren, (in order of appearance) Amber, Noah, David, Ben and Matthew.